Leadership Lessons I Learned on the Links:

72 Ways to Par the Course of Business and Life

Book One of Four

Leadership Lessons 1 - 18

by

Tom Hinton

Published by:

Blue Carriage Publishing Company

Post Office Box 880774

San Diego, CA 92168-0774

Leadership Lessons I Learned on the Links:
72 Ways to Par the Course of Business and Life

Book One of Four
Leadership Lessons: 1 - 18

Blue Carriage Publishing Company is Pleased that *Leadership Lessons I Learned on the Links* is the first business book to be published in the New Millennium, January 1, 2001. Congratulations to author Tom Hinton.

First Edition, Blue Carriage Publishing Company, January 1, 2001

The Library of Congress Cataloging-in-Publication Data
Hinton, Tom
Leadership Lessons I Learned on the Links: 72 Ways to Par the Course of Business and Life, Book One / by Tom Hinton
ISBN 0-9703036-0-2

Manufactured in the United States of America 10 9 8 7 6 5

Acknowledgments

One sunny morning in the winter of 1995, I was walking along the 13th fairway of the Mt. Woodson County Club near San Diego with Fred Selzer. Fred was a guest-in-residence from Kansas City. We would often take early morning walks together and liberate lost golf balls in the bushes and rugged hillsides along the lush fairways of Mt. Woodson. It was not uncommon for us to find 20 or more golf balls on our morning walk.

I shared with Fred my idea for a new book that would feature a number of lessons I had learned on the golf course. I thought these lessons were applicable to business and life, as well as golf. Fred encouraged me to move forward on this project. What you are now reading is the first book in a series of four dedicated to the 72 leadership lessons I've learned on the links.

The constant affirmation of any idea is vital to its growth and fruition. I am indebted to the many people who showed me the way and supported this book from concept to completion.

I owe a special thanks to the many members of Mt. Woodson Country Club for their ideas, support, and review of the manuscripts throughout its many stages. Among those members are Rick and Penny Sullivan; Jon and Joann Toolson; Scott Welsh, the head pro at La Costa; Harding Dawe; Larry Antoinette; Rick Kline; and Jim Gleason.

Thanks are also due to Steve Dawe and the Mt. Woodson Group. I also want to thank many of my clients including Don Moschenross, who made me three excellent wedge clubs and proved that even a perfect club in the wrong hands will not produce birdies and pars. Also, I appreciate the support of several people from the California Quality Awards program including Dave Richey, Dempsey Copeland, Chris Ensign, Dave Lehmann, Malcolm Franks, and a special thanks to Mike Maslak, CEO of North Island Federal Credit Union, for his initial support of this project. Gary Plantz of the *San Diego Business Journal*, has been instrumental in helping me market this book. Alicia Pettersen provided the photo-sketches; and Angie Roberts, of Graphic Details, labored many hours to typeset and format this book and design the cover. Thank you!

I want to pay a special tribute to our late friend, Bob Bennett, who passed away before this book could be published. He inspired us with his dry Texan wit, and he always saw the cup on every green as half-full.

Finally, I am very grateful to the many business leaders and companies around the world that have supported this book. Through their support they have contributed to the financial endowment of the Leadership Links Foundation, which is dedicated to mentoring our future leaders through the principles and the game of golf. My personal commitment is to donate 50 percent of the proceeds from every book sold to the Leadership Links Foundation.

In an era when our youth cries out for direction and attention, I hope this book will inspire adults around the world to donate one day a month to mentoring our future leaders so that we can continue to enjoy the liberties and freedoms we all cherish.

Table of Contents
LEADERSHIP LESSONS I LEARNED ON THE LINKS
72 Ways to Par the Course of Business & Life
Book One of Four
By: Tom Hinton

LEADERSHIP LESSONS I LEARNED ON THE LINKS:
72 Ways to Par the Course of Business and Life

Book One
by Tom Hinton

"Golf is of games the most mystical,
the least earthbound
the one wherein the walls between us and the supernatural are rubbed thinnest."

– John Updike

"Golf is more exacting than racing, cards, speculation or matrimony. In almost all other games you pit yourself against a mortal foe; in golf it is yourself against the world: no human being stays your progress as you drive your ball over the face of the globe."

– Arnold Haultain
The Mystery of Golf

"Golf is a game to teach you about the messages from within, about the subtle voices of the body-mind. And once you understand them you can more clearly see your 'hamartia', the ways in which your approach to the game reflects your entire life. Nowhere does a man go so naked."

– Michael Murphy
Golf in the Kingdom

Golf

Golf is a science, the study of a lifetime, in which you may exhaust yourself but never your subject. It is a contest, a duel, or a melee, calling for courage, skill, strategy, and self-control. It is a test of temper, a trial of honor, a revealer of character. It affords a chance to play the man and act the gentleman. It means going into God's out-of-doors, getting close to nature, fresh air, exercise, a sweeping away of mental cobwebs, genuine recreation of tired tissues. It is a cure for care, an antidote to worry. It includes companionship with friends, social intercourse, opportunities for courtesy, kindliness and generosity to an opponent. It promotes not only physical health but moral force.

– David R. Forgan, St. Andrews, Scotland

The Greatest Game

Golf is deceptively simple and
endlessly complicated.
A child can play it well and a grown
man can never master it.

Any single round of it is full of
unexpected triumphs
And seemingly perfect shots
that end in disaster.

It is almost a science, yet it is a puzzle
without an answer.
It is gratifying and tantalizing,
precise and unpredictable.

It requires complete concentration
and total relaxation.
It satisfies the soul and frustrates
the intellect.

It is, at the same time, rewarding
and maddening.
And it is, without a doubt, the greatest game
mankind has ever invented.

– Anonymous

The Character of the Man

Golf is the infallible test. The man who can go into a patch of rough alone, with the knowledge that only God is watching him, and play his ball where it lies, is the man who will serve you faithfully and well.

The man who can smile bravely when his putt is diverted by one of those beastly wormcasts is pure golf right through. But, the man who is hasty, unbalanced and violent on the links will display the same qualities in the wider field of everyday life."

– P. G. Wodehouse
Golf Without Tears

A note to the reader from the author about the use of gender terminology in this book:

Throughout this book, I use the masculine gender. I realize that many women enjoy golf and they, too, are capable leaders. However, I've chosen to use the masculine form because a simple and inclusive gender terminology doesn't yet exist. I offer this explanation in the hope that no one is offended by my efforts to simplify the text. – Tom Hinton

INTRODUCTION:
ABOUT LEADERSHIP AND GOLF

This book is the first in a series of four volumes I have authored about two popular subjects that dominate most business conversations today – leadership and golf.

Commerce and the game of golf have been entwined for more than 500 years. Ever since that day in 1457, when King James II of Scotland temporarily banned the game because it interfered with the practice of archery and his country's commerce, golf's popularity has grown.

Golf and leadership are inseparable because the game of golf, like leadership, is a test through which we are constantly challenged to push beyond our self-imposed limits. As with business and sports, both the leader and the golfer are measured by their results. The business leader's performance is measured by the numbers on the company's balance sheet. The golfer's performance is measured by the number in the little box on his scorecard. Sam Snead once quipped, "Nobody ever asked me how I looked, just what I shot." The elementary challenge facing every leader and golfer is this: "How do I achieve a winning performance?"

Over the years, I have learned many valuable leadership lessons on the links that have helped me to grow as a person and as an entrepreneur. This book features 18 leadership lessons I learned from an early mentor, Jack Rudabee, during my high school and college years while I caddied for him at his country club in Bethesda, Maryland. As a result of that powerful, life-altering experience I grew to appreciate, respect, and love the game.

In fact, I think golf is the most challenging game ever created because you have to learn to win by yourself. There's no one else to take your shots or help you overcome your mental anxieties. A person's failures on the links cannot be blamed on the golf gremlins or distractions. Tom Watson said it best, "In golf, you have to learn to win by yourself. That's why it's the greatest game. You win by yourself and you win for yourself."

Years ago, I remember reading Walter Hagen's commentary on winning. It hung on the conference room wall in Jack Rudabee's office in Chevy Chase, Maryland. It read, "No one remembers who finished second." That one sentence was a motivating force in Jack Rudabee's life. He had it printed, framed, and distributed to his employees, customers, and suppliers. Next to it was a statement made by another golf legend, Jack Nicklaus. It read, "Ask yourself how many shots you would have saved if you never lost your temper, never got down on yourself, always developed a strategy before you hit, and always played within your own capabilities."

I offer you these leadership lessons in the same spirit that Jack Rudabee gave them to me – as a way to develop our leadership abilities and the lives of those people we touch and influence.

What Is Leadership?

Leadership, like golf, is an enigma. It is one of those subjects you can talk about all day long but, in the final analysis, it remains elusive and open to many interpretations.

Jack Rudabee told me that leadership isn't defined by one's title, rank, or office. These things are merely the symbols and trappings of leaders. Leadership is about one's ability to advance people and organizations through ideas. Every great leader from Julius Caesar to Churchill had the ability to inspire and motivate people based on an idea. Leadership is an evolving discipline and art form that requires a person to learn and listen as much as it requires someone to teach and talk.

I define leadership as the ability to help individuals and organizations *surpass* themselves. The key word in my definition is *surpass* because leadership is ultimately about transforming people – emotionally and mentally – from what they are to what they can become. For, it is only through the act of leading people that ideas are born and nurtured to fruition; that products and services reach the marketplace; that companies become successful; and, the world becomes a better place. Leadership is also about results – finding ways to continuously improve and raise the bar in an effort to achieve a winning performance.

Similarly, golf is a game that demands from us a commitment to continuously practice, play, and improve our skills if we expect to improve our results – that is, our score. If we fail to do the things that improve our results, such as practice frequently and play the game often, our results will suffer. Ben Hogan, one of America's greatest golfers and teachers of the game, said "Every day you miss playing or practicing is one day longer it takes to be good."

Likewise, when we fail to practice our leadership skills, our ability to inspire and grow people and organizations weakens and, eventually, wilts. Golf, like leadership, also reflects the cycle of life. Golf pro Peter Jacobsen observed this fact. He said, "No matter how good a game you shoot, the next day you have to go back out there to the first tee and begin all over again and make yourself into something." This is why leadership, like golf, is the ultimate test of a person's ability to adapt, change, and manage outcomes under very difficult situations.

Leaders, like golfers, come in all sizes, shapes, styles, colors, genders, and creeds. There is no single mold for greatness. I believe that those who want to excel and achieve greatness in their lifetime have the power to do so. While each person has his or her own personal formula for success, many of the leadership lessons in this book are the same lessons applied by great men and women around the world who have rightfully earned the title of "enlightened leaders."

This book, first and foremost, is about your ability to mentor and lead people, better manage yourself, and achieve your goals – on and off the golf course. It is but one proven path you can travel to discover the way to genuine power; and in the process become a person whose life is successful and significant.

MY MENTOR AND TEACHER

Every successful leader and golfer I have met attributes much of their success to a host of teachers, mentors, and coaches. I am no different in this respect.

At the impressionable age of fifteen, I began my formal learning about leadership and its powerful connection to golf. While living in Maryland a high school friend, whose family belonged to a prominent country club, encouraged me to join him as a caddie during our freshman year. Soon thereafter, on a Saturday afternoon in late May, I began a relationship with my greatest mentor and teacher, Jack Rudabee, that would last a lifetime. Jack was a very successful businessman who earned his fortune in construction, real estate investments, and restaurant and hotel franchises.

Jack considered the golf course his laboratory for learning. It was from him that I learned the leadership lessons you'll read in this series. It was Jack who first taught me the familiar Zen saying, "When the student is ready, the teacher will appear."

After meeting him for the first time – I was ready.

In college, Jack Rudabee discovered through golf a game that taught him how to succeed in business and life. Through golf, he was able to master the science of people and build lifelong relationships with people from all walks of life. Wherever he traveled Jack Rudabee had many friends. Through golf he was able to communicate and speak a common language with people around the world. Jack believed that golf and being a Rotarian could open any door on the planet.

Jack never hired a key associate or allowed anyone to conduct important business with his company until he had first played golf with him. Their ability to shoot a low score wasn't important to Jack. What was important to Jack was that he used golf as a way to gauge a person's character and integrity. Jack believed he could learn more about a person during one round of golf than he could by interviewing him in an office. As Grantland Rice once quipped, "Eighteen holes of golf will teach you more about a person than eighteen years of dealing with him across a desk."

Jack celebrated his 52nd birthday two weeks before we met. He studied Liberal Arts and Business at Boston College. Jack lettered in basketball, and football. After graduating from Boston College, he played professional football in Baltimore for two years. When World War II erupted, Jack enlisted in the army and shipped out to Europe. During the Battle of the Bulge, he was wounded and that put an end to his professional football career.

He spent four months in a hospital bed in Paris recuperating from the bullet that ripped through his lower back muscles and left him numb on his right side. When he returned to the United States, he continued his physical therapy. Golf became a regular part of his daily exercise program at Walter Reed Hospital in Washington, D.C.

It was at this point in his life that he began to re-think his reason for living. He came to the conclusion that a meaningful life was best defined as not only achieving success, but also doing something significant. According to Jack, the only thing of any real worth and value a person leaves behind is his legacy. He said to me, "I want to be remembered for my significance on earth, not how much money I earned."

Eventually, Jack worked his way into a senior executive position for a large commercial construction company in the Washington, D.C. area. In 1956, he decided to leave the comfort and financial security of his employer to establish his own real estate development business. He began by building homes in Maryland and Virginia. He believed in his goal of making peoples' dreams come true. He wanted to be a builder of good things in his life – and he was.

Management According to Rudabee:

Jack's management philosophy could best be described as "performance-driven." Jack understood that each person was unique and different and, therefore, there were many ways to achieve a winning performance. Jack really didn't care how someone got the right results as long as they did it honestly, fairly, and played as a team. On Jack Rudabee's team, there was room for superstars, but not prima donnas.

> "I am an optimist. It does not seem too much use being anything else."
>
> – Winston Churchill

His tactics on the golf course were no different than the way he managed his business dealings. Clearly, his management style was designed around winning. But, in the process, he was determined to win fairly and have fun. And, he did!

The day after I graduated from college, Jack Rudabee invited me to visit with him at his country club. He said he had a special graduation present for me and suggested I bring a thick notebook. I took his advice and during the next two days, Jack unwrapped one of the greatest gifts I've ever received.

A soft spring rain was falling lightly on the lush green fairways when I arrived at the club. It had been almost seven years to the day when I first strapped on his golf bag and caddied for him.

Jack and I retreated to the ivy-covered porch that skirted the clubhouse and overlooked the 10th hole. Our first in-depth conversation began mid-morning on the clubhouse patio and continued until the sun slipped behind the soggy pines and wet willow trees that bordered the 18th fairway. We began with a round of Cherry Cokes, our favorite soft drink, and a warm bowl of Campbell's chicken noodle soup. It hit the spot. And then Jack

"If you can't break 80, you have no business playing golf. If you can break 80, you have no business!"

–Old British saying

began to teach me the 72 leadership lessons he had learned during a lifetime of playing golf and dealing with people.

Throughout that afternoon and into the twilight hours, I sat mesmerized as Jack began to reveal these brief, but powerful, leadership lessons that have guided me to success. He spoke to me about his life, business, the art of leadership, and the game of golf. He encouraged me to take copious notes. I did. I preserved that spiral-bound notebook all through the years never knowing it would serve as the basis for a book on leadership and golf. Although some of the pages have faded and the handwriting is smeared and discolored from rain drops, the essence of his words and the leadership lessons he shared with me that spring weekend are still vivid in my mind.

Jack began our session by defining the 18 attributes of a leader.

18 Attributes of a Leader

Jack believed that every person who aspires to success must master the 18 attributes of a leader. He developed his list over many years of being in business and dealing with all types of people in a variety of challenging situations.

The 18 Attributes of a Leader, as Jack defined them, are:

1. Courage.

The leader develops the ability to overcome self-doubts and fears, and take risks even in the face of difficult odds. Without courage, a person is paralyzed and unable to act.

2. Clarity of Purpose.

The leader has a clear reason for being and doing what he does. Although most leaders are dreamers first and visionaries second, all leaders have translated their dreams into goals.

3. *Written Goals.*

The difference between goals and dreams is that goals are set in writing. The leader imagines a desired end-result and establishes a goal that inspires people to reach beyond their self-imposed limits. The leader reviews his goals daily and commits them to memory.

4. *Focus and Determination.*

The leader has the power of concentration and stays focused. He does not become distracted nor lose sight of his objective. A lack of focus is the primary reason most people never reach their full potential. The leader is also determined. Jack believed that much of success can be attributed to a leader's conviction that his plans are achievable despite the naysayers and pessimists. The leader perseveres down the fairways of life, always focused on hitting the ball into the cup.

5. *Love of People.*

The leader accomplishes his purpose and goals through, and with, people. The leader develops a genuine love for people and, in doing so, earns their respect and trust.

6. *Integrity.*

At the core of a leader's value system is integrity. People will follow a leader they trust. The best way for a leader to earn someone's trust is to honor his words and promises – that is, living what you say and doing what you ask of others.

7. *Respect for All Living Things.*

The leader understands and appreciates that all living things on this planet are inter-related and connected by a higher power. A person cannot fully respect himself if he does not value all living things and their role in our extended universe.

8. *The Ability to Communicate.*

A leader develops the ability to think clearly and express himself eloquently in order to espouse ideas that inspire other people to embrace his vision and goals. This is the heart of communication.

9. *A Listening Heart.*

The leader, like old King Solomon from the Biblical days, has the gift of a listening heart. He seeks first to understand, then to be understood. It is important for the leader to suppress his own feelings and emotions in order to hear in his heart what others are trying to tell him. The leader does not judge solely by what he hears; rather, he reflects on the message instead of the emotions wrapped around the person's words.

10. *A Sense of Humor.*

The leader is able to smile, laugh, and enjoy his way to the top. Without a sense of humor, it is a very steep climb to the top and a bruising fall to the bottom.

11. *Self-confidence.*

The leader believes in himself and, by his example, he inspires confidence, support, and trust from others. The leader separates confidence from arrogance by knowing his limits and accepting his imperfections. The leader understands that while there are no secrets to success, there are systems to success. The leader inspires his followers to pursue the path along which they will discover their own system to success. Jack's favorite definition of confidence was the fisherman who goes after Moby Dick in a rowboat with a long rope, a harpoon, and a jar of tartar sauce!

12. Fairness.

The leader understands that fairness has more to do with making people feel special than it does with enforcing policies, rules, and procedures. Fairness means everybody has a chance to succeed. The leader never denies someone the opportunity to succeed because of his own inadequacies, biases, prejudices, or limitations. The leader doesn't hide behind his weaknesses. He uses them as a way to assess his performance, overcome his imperfections, and act fairly in his treatment of others.

13. Innovation.

The leader has imagination. The leader sees the possibilities for the future and encourages his people to think outside the box and dream big. The leader knows that good ideas can only reach fruition if he fosters an environment that champions innovation, encourages uninhibited thinking, and promotes unlimited possibilities for the future. Teamwork is the leader's tool for harvesting innovation.

14. Decisiveness.

The leader acts by making decisions carefully, and in a timely manner, so that opportunities are not wasted. The leader also is slow to reverse his decisions once they are made because he has conviction and determination.

15. Negotiating Skills.

The leader understands that givers gain. But the leader also understands that everybody wants something. This is the heart of every negotiation. The leader tries to give others what they want without giving away what he needs or cannot afford to do without on his journey to achieving his mission.

16. Salesmanship.

The leader is always selling something – an idea, a theme, a product, a service, or a goal. But, most importantly, the leader sells himself. The genuine leader sells himself by articulating his purpose and achieving his goals without compromising his integrity in the process.

17. Physical and Emotional Stamina.

The leader is physically and mentally ready to do battle. This is why the leader eats right, sleeps well, exercises regularly, and does not abuse himself through stress, worry, alcohol, drugs, or other vices and excuses.

18. Anticipation.

The leader anticipates the future. He can smell opportunity in the air. The leader, like a chess player, anticipates best-case and worse-case scenarios and then prepares for these possibilities. The leader is always ready to act and take advantage of a favorable situation. Although he can be spontaneous, the leader doesn't shoot from the hip. He is calculating and methodical in his approach to seizing the opportunity.

Following this introduction, Jack revealed 18 of the 72 leadership lessons he would share with me that weekend in May. Here they are, in the order he gave them to me.

Leadership Lesson: #1

KNOW WHY YOU PLAY THE GAME

The leader knows why he plays the game. Knowing one's purpose is the foundation for all success in life.

In order for people to excel at something meaningful in life, they must know *why* they're doing it. They must believe in their purpose and understand what drives them to be successful. Knowing the *why* sustains them through the ups-and-downs along their journey.

This lesson is applicable in business, life, and golf. Only you can decide your purpose and why you play the game the way you do.

Most people don't give this question much thought. In fact, most people just show up on the first tee of life and swing away. A lack of preparation and forethought begets mediocre results. Consider this fact. Most people spend more time planning their summer vacation than they do defining their life purpose. Jack believed that defining one's purpose in life is "an act of faith" because it requires people to believe in themselves. He said, "defining one's purpose is the first step a person must take if they want to transform their dreams, wishes, and fantasies into reality."

"Have a clear vision of the target and focus on it. Have a well-defined purpose for existence, a reason for being, and an ultimate goal in life."
–Bobby Clampett

In the world of business, as in the game of golf, the most successful leaders strive to reach their ultimate level of competence. The ultimate level of competence is the attainment of wisdom. Wisdom does not come solely from the books you read and the people you meet. A leader must experience life fully in order to appreciate the lessons it teaches and to garner wisdom.

I define wisdom as the ability to make the right decision the first time.

Wisdom is accomplished as a result of a four-step process. First, we gather data. Secondly, our brain naturally converts data into information and sorts it and stores it in our mind. Once we have information, we proceed to the third step which is knowledge. Data combined with information creates the potential for knowledge. Finally, the fourth step, wisdom is achieved when the leader is able to use his knowledge to make the right decision the first time.

Jack Rudabee was very clear about his purpose on and off the golf links. He set aside fifteen minutes at the beginning of each day as his solitary time to reflect on his purpose and establish his goals for the day. It was also his chance to clear away any thoughts that conflicted with his purpose. Jack had a powerful expression that I still recite whenever I find myself not focused on my desired outcome. It goes, "If you want to change your results, you must change your behavior. If you want to change your behavior, then you must change the way you think. And, if you want to change the way you think, you must define your purpose and create new goals." By focusing your thoughts on your purpose and goals, you can achieve significant results in a short period of time.

Jack understood that everybody has a unique purpose on this planet. Our greatest challenge in life is to discover our purpose and then put our talents to work and achieve it. Some people are called as inventors and teachers; others are destined as salespeople or parents. No one's purpose is more important than another's. We are a global community bound together by the richness of our talents, knowledge, diversity, and interests. Everyone has a meaningful role to play. But, the most difficult question you must answer in order to attain significance is this: "What is my purpose in life?"

In July, after I had caddied for Jack Rudabee several times, he began to ask me questions such as, "So, Tom, why do you play the game of golf?" I responded as any fifteen-year-old boy would, by telling him it was fun, and I enjoyed the outdoors and the relaxed environment. But I could tell by Jack's facial expressions that he was not impressed with my answers. And so, he continued to press me from time to time with introspective questions.

One summer afternoon, I summoned up the courage to ask him why he played the game? I was not prepared for his reply. In fact, it took me nearly twenty years to fully appreciate his answer. Jack said, "I play the game of golf for many reasons. But the most compelling reason is this. Through golf, I am able to play out my personal struggle between the forces of *genuine power and ego power.*" He could tell from my expression that I hadn't a clue about what he meant; and so, he elaborated.

Jack told me the greatest struggle a human being faces is to accomplish something significant in his life. He noted anybody could achieve success, but very few people attain significance in their life. The reason why few leaders attain significance is because they succumb to the forces of *ego power* instead of pushing themselves and testing their limits; which is required in order to achieve *genuine power.*

Jack defined *genuine power* as "The ability to act with a wisdom that is based upon tested knowledge and with honorable intentions even in the face of opposition." He believed the attainment of *genuine power* is the primary purpose of our being. It is what we must strive for on earth because *genuine power* is unlimited and it is based on our self-fulfillment and commitment to achieving good.

Genuine power is attained when we let go of our basic fears and insecurities and move beyond the limitations of our five senses. It is the natural, fluid swing in golf as opposed to the rehearsed, controlled, inhibited swing. It is the intuitive decisions we make in business, rather than those sterilized decisions that are reviewed by three layers of management, sanitized for political correctness, and justified by reams of data and information from unaffected and disinterested third parties.

Jack defined *ego power* as "the individual ego's need to control events and outcomes." This includes our self-power to control our environment – and those within it – as well as having power over what can be seen, felt, smelled, tasted, or heard. In other words, *ego power* dictates that we must have control over our five senses and those persons who influence what we see, hear, touch, feel, and smell.

The leader's struggle to attain *genuine power* is all the more difficult because *ego power* is easier to grasp and, therefore, more appealing to most people.

Ego power is driven largely by our most dominant fears and insecurities. When we are not "in control," we fear the consequences. When operating from the grip of *ego power*, we seldom make the best decisions – in business or personal matters – because we do not trust ourselves or our organization to succeed. We lack confidence. Although many of our decisions

"Singleness of purpose! That must be our attitude towards every stroke we play."

–Leslie Schon
The Psychology of Golf

might achieve the desired outcomes, they are inherently flawed because they are made out of context; that is, we are driven by all the wrong motivators, including control and fear. *Ego power* is merely a quick-fix for human beings in search of fulfillment.

Many executives and managers in the private and public sector rely on *ego power* to direct their organizations because this is how they were taught. It is also the reason why most organizations under-perform. This is why professional golfer Jack Burke Jr. observed, "the average golfer doesn't play golf; he attacks it." Ironically, most managers attack a problem because they are ego-driven to achieve results. They are unaware that their decisions and management methods are based on the principles of *ego power.*

In contrast, *genuine power* is the more difficult of the two powers to acquire because it requires a transformation within one's self – from what we are to the ideal of what we want to become. Completing this transformation is what makes an enlightened leader. No one can claim to be an enlightened leader until he or she has acquired *genuine power.* And, as Jack Rudabee taught me, it is a long and difficult journey because it requires total focus, determination, and an ability to change. Few people understand these transformational steps and even fewer take them. But, for those who undertake this transformational challenge, it is a rewarding one because it leads to lasting fulfillment and joy in life.

Genuine power is attained in three ways. First, it is attained when you are able to love. A heart that cannot love, cannot lead. Secondly, it is attained when you have respect for all living things in our universe. A person who does not revere life cannot fully value himself. And, thirdly, it is attained when you perceive meaningfulness and purpose in even the smallest details on Earth. Someone who cannot see meaning and purpose in the smallest of Earth's treasurers is blind to the blades of grass that make the lush fairways and greens of our lives.

For greater insight on the human struggle for power, I recommend you read Gary Zukav's popular, best-selling book, *The Seat of the Soul* (Simon & Schuster).

Leadership Lesson #1 Learned:

Be clear about your purpose in everything you do. Define your purpose in action-oriented words. Commit yourself to doing something that will consume your thoughts and energies; something you feel passionate about in life. Have the courage to stay the course and overcome your ego needs. Strive to attain genuine power. *When you know why you "play the game", everything is much clearer to you.*

Leadership Lesson #2:
THE LEADER IS ALWAYS ON A MISSION

The leader's mission compliments his purpose and principles.

In Laurie Beth Jones' insightful book, *The Path,* she observes that every great leader – from Lincoln to Gandhi – has a viable mission. The leader achieves his mission by defining his purpose and articulating the principles by which he lives.

Jack Rudabee taught me that a leader's mission requires a clear vision, attainable goals, and specific tasks. I refer to this approach as the "MVGT System." As *The Path* reveals, Lincoln's mission was to preserve the Union. Gandhi's mission was the independence of India through non-violent means. Jack Rudabee's mission was to create harmonious living communities for families.

"A plan of attack must be sound, based on solid, well-tested principles. We must think hard and constructively and then we must act quickly while the plan is fresh in mind. It is fatal to change the plan half-way through the operation."
–Eric M. Prain
Live Hands

Jack told me that in order to define one's principles, a person must consider four factors. They are your beliefs, values, attitudes, and behavior. Everything we think, say, and do is a direct result of these four factors. Henry Ford best captured the essence of principles when he said, "Whether you think you can or you think you can't, you're right!" Ford understood that much of success is tied to *how* we think and *what* we think.

Anyone who has achieved something significant in his life knows the importance of believing in one's idea and self. According to the “Father of Positive Thinking,” Norman Vincent Peale, it is practically impossible to accomplish something worthwhile without first believing it is doable.

Our beliefs are the most difficult to challenge and change because we acquire them at an early age. Psychiatrists tell us that by the age of seven years, most children have formed eighty percent of their beliefs. Certainly, we are a product of our environment – for better or for worse. The beliefs and values we learn from our family, friends, and teachers in our formative years shape our self-image and how well or poorly we interact with society.

The most difficult aspect of coming to grips with our beliefs, values, attitudes, and behavior is subjecting them to careful scrutiny. This is a critical test for every successful leader because it forces the leader to re-examine his life and what he believes in. And yet, every great leader completes this extraordinary introspection during his life.

One way to change your behavior is to change the way you think. This requires you to put your beliefs on trial. You must challenge them and test them against other standards. If your beliefs go unchallenged, you will always see things the same way. This perception limits your thinking and shuts out the possibility of new, innovative thinking.

In 1949, Ben Hogan, one of the greatest golfers and teachers of the game, suffered massive injuries in a car accident while driving with his wife to a tournament. He collided head-on with a tour bus that was attempting to pass a truck on a foggy two-lane highway near Van Horn, Texas. Hogan's quick thinking saved his wife, but nearly cost him his own life. Many people, including several of the doctors who worked feverishly to save Ben Hogan's life, thought he would never be able to walk again, let alone play golf. But Ben Hogan proved them wrong. He did not accept their pessimistic prognosis. Instead, Hogan began to rebuild his debilitated body. In January, 1950, less than eight months after his near-fatal car accident, Hogan stunned the golf world as he competed in the Los Angeles Open. Despite a remarkable comeback performance, Hogan lost to Sam Snead in a playoff.

But even more amazing was Hogan's performance in the 1950 U.S. Open. That June, Hogan hung on to tie the leaders in regulation play. In the ensuing 18-hole playoff, Hogan showed the world of golf what determination and persistence were all about by winning the tournament in remarkable fashion.

As he hobbled up the 18th fairway, barely able to carry himself on his crippled legs, the gallery gave Hogan a thunderous ovation. It was their way of congratulating and saluting Ben Hogan on one of the most remarkable comebacks any golfer had achieved.

As a leader, consider your beliefs, values, attitudes, and behavior. Will they allow you to render a Hogan-like performance?

To achieve one's mission, the leader must have a clear sense of who he is and why he exists. This clarity of purpose is defined by the four cornerstones of the MVGT formula:

1. A *mission* Statement defines your overall reason for living. It is brief, to the point, and can be easily memorized.

2. A *vision* Statement defines who you are, where you are going, and how you will get there.

3. *Goals* are ideas directed to a desired result. Your goals should be intermediate benchmarks – like mile posts along the highway to your destination – that are specific, measurable, attainable, relevant to your mission, and timely (deadlines).

4. *Tasks* define each primary step you must take in order to achieve your goals.

Let me give you an example of how someone can achieve their dream through the "mission, vision, goals, and tasks" system.

There was a member at the country club named Scotty. When Scotty retired at age 58, he embarked on a new goal, to break 80 by his sixtieth birthday. Whenever he played the game of golf, Scotty was totally focused on achieving his dream. He shared his dream with everyone.

It was no secret. He took lessons. He practiced. He played golf at least twice a week. And, he prayed fervently to the golf gods. But the best score Scotty every recorded was 82. Try as he might, Scotty just couldn't break 80 with an honest score.

The week before his 60th birthday, Jack Rudabee invited Scotty to a round of golf on his birthday. Since Jack regularly broke the magical 80 mark, he thought he could inspire Scotty to do the same. I was one of the caddies that Labor Day weekend. What I witnessed was an extraordinary testimony to the power of the MVGT formula which Jack espoused.

Jack invited Scotty to have breakfast with him at the country club the day before his birthday to formulate a strategy for breaking 80. When Scotty questioned the need for a "strategy session," Jack reminded him of golf pro Bob Toski's comment. "Most golfers prepare for disaster," said Toski, "but a good golfer prepares for success." Scotty agreed to Jack's strategy session.

At breakfast, they wrote down on two napkins Scotty's "Mission, Vision, Goals, and Tasks" for breaking 80 the next day. They reviewed in detail each hole and designed a strategy to score par or better. Then, they computed Scotty's score based on their calculations and strategy.

Scotty now believed he could actually shoot a 78, based on this plan. Prior to this session, Scotty had only dreamed about breaking 80.

With a renewed sense of commitment and a written strategy stuffed in his back pocket, Scotty set off the next day to play his birthday round. After nine holes, Scotty was one over with a score of 37. He was elated. The best he'd ever shot on the front nine was 39. He was following his game strategy and it was working for him. Scotty's foursome quietly encouraged him without adding any pressure. Jack counseled Scotty not to worry by reminding him of what Bobby Jones had to say about pressure. Jones once quipped, "Some people think they are concentrating when they're merely worrying." Scotty chuckled and played on with a renewed sense of confidence.

Approaching the demanding par five, 18th hole, with its dog-leg left and stream cutting across the fairway, Scotty only needed a bogey to break 80. In the past, this was the hole that had always beaten Scotty. Jack knew this and casually reminded Scotty of his Mission and their strategy for paring Number 18. Scotty faded his tee shot into perfect position some 205 yards down the fairway. His second shot carried the stream, leaving him a comfortable 160 yard shot to the green. His third shot plugged on the green just twenty feet from the pin. Although he missed his birdie putt, Scotty was "inside the leather" and tapped in for a well-deserved par – his fifteenth of the day – and a record low score of 78. He was greeted with high fives and hugs from everyone. It was the best birthday present anyone

"Conductors of great symphony orchestras do not play every musical instrument; yet, through leadership, the ultimate production is an expressive and unified combination of tones."
–Thomas D. Bailey

could have given him. Ironically, he gave it to himself simply by creating a plan, owning that plan, and executing the plan using the MVGT formula Jack had helped him design.

Later that day, I asked Jack about his experience with Scotty and what he thought had made the difference for Scotty's winning performance that morning. Jack told me that Scotty had always dreamed about breaking 80, but he never put his dreams on paper. "For Scotty," Jack said, "breaking 80 was a dream, but never a goal. But once Scotty set it in writing, his dream became realistic, attainable, and visible to him. He could finally picture success in his mind."

I've always remembered that experience because it created in my mind a powerful picture of what people can accomplish when they have clarity of purpose and commit in writing to achieving their goals through the MVGT formula.

Leadership Lesson #2 Learned:

To realize success, first determine your purpose.

Then put your mission statement in writing. Next, outline a detailed plan for success that includes your vision, goals, and tasks. Review it twice daily. Revise your plan yearly. Always track and measure your progress on a daily, weekly, and monthly basis. Remember, it's no different than keeping score in golf. You must count each stroke on every hole in order to arrive at the final tally.

Leadership Lesson #3:
UNDERSTAND THE RULES OF THE GAME

The leader understands the rules of the game. He respects the rules and abides by them even when no one is looking.

Every aspect of life has rules. The leader who knows the rules and understands how to interpret or apply the rules of a game, holds a distinct advantage over his competitors. There are several important benefits to understanding the rules of a game. First, knowing the rules prevents you from making mistakes and embarrassing yourself. For example, in a club championship tournament, I remember a player was penalized for picking up a pine cone that he had inadvertently kicked into a sand trap. Without thinking, he picked up the pine cone before he played his shot out of the bunker and suffered a severe two-stroke penalty. USGA Rules clearly state that you cannot remove a loose impediment in a hazard before your stroke is played.

Another benefit of knowing the rules is it keeps your opponents honest. Who will ever forget the 1968 Masters Tournament when Roberto de Vincenzo was deprived of his Masters Title because he signed an incorrect scorecard. His playing partner, Tommy Aaron, who was keeping de Vincenzo's scorecard, inadvertently wrote down a 4 instead of the correct score of 3 during Roberto's final round. When Roberto signed the card and submitted it, the tournament officials had no choice but to award Bob Goalby first place. A dejected de Vincenzo was awarded second place. Ironically, the Argentinian received mega-dollars in corporate endorsements as well as thousands of cards and letters from admiring fans who applauded his integrity.

The British historian, Lord Macaulay, wrote, "The measure of a man's true character is what he would do if he knew he would never be found out." Integrity is one of the greatest virtues on the links. It ranks #6 on Jack Rudabee's list of the 18 Attributes of a Leader. No other sport allows players to police themselves to the extent golf does. In every major professional sport there are referees, umpires, or overseers who enforce the rules. Golf is the only game in which the player is both scorekeeper and referee. Still, there are rules in golf and those rules must be fairly interpreted and obeyed. By knowing the rules, you can be sure that fairness, decency, and common courtesy on the links will be extended to you.

In the world of business, the rules are somewhat more complicated because they are clouded by legal interpretations and each person's ethical standards. But, the genuine leader is guided by a higher rule. That rule is a leader's own sense of fairness. I refer to this as a leader's "intentions." It is through the leader's intentions that

"You might as well praise a man for not robbing a bank as to praise him for playing by the rules."
–Bobby Jones

"I have come to think that a person grows in his regard for the rules as he improves his game. The best players come to love golf so much they hate to see the game violated in any way."

–Michael Murphy, Author
Golf in the Kingdom

he defines his true character. This is one of the primary differences between a genuine leader and the ego-driven leader.

While everyone makes decisions based on his beliefs, values, and attitudes, ultimately, the genuine leader allows his behavior to be determined by his intentions. The leader, by his very character, chooses to do what is right and fair.

The leader doesn't compromise his integrity by loosely interpreting certain rules to suit his circumstances. In golf, a player cannot ignore the rule book without compromising his integrity. It says a great deal about a person's principles or lack thereof.

The rules of golf, like a traffic signal, exist for everyone. They control the ebb and flow of the game as well as any special circumstances that arise. A leader understands the rules of the game and interprets them fairly whether they apply to him or others. This is why golf is a game of honor. To openly lie or cheat about your score is to dishonor yourself and the game you play.

Over the years I have learned the value of

"The more often your opponent quotes the rules of golf, the greater the certainty that he cheats!"
–W. C. Fields

"Any kind of knowledge gives a certain amount of power. A knowledge of details has served in many a crisis. A knowledge of details has often caught an error before it became a catastrophe."
–Aimee Buchanan

knowing the rules. I have observed how respect for and knowledge of the rules in business have helped certain leaders gain a competitive edge, while those people who hold the rules in contempt, or try to circumvent the rules, have selfishly brought unnecessary suffering and hardship on their companies, customers and employees. Some ego-driven executives are so arrogant they believe they can violate statutes and get away with it. But, eventually, their lack of respect for the rules ensures their downfall.

On the fairways and greens, I have learned that the laws of the universe and respect for nature also apply to golfers. For example, I have watched how professional golfers and conscientious duffers carefully maneuver around flower beds or shrubs in an effort not to trample them when retrieving their misdirected ball. A leader's respect for these same laws of the universe will come full circle and reward them. Recently, I read the biography of a young business executive who was offered a promotion as president of a company and a seat on the board of directors under the condition he vote the way he was told by the chairman. He refused the promotion and quit. But, as soon as his colleagues heard of his decision, they rallied around him by quitting their jobs, starting a new company, and creating their own highly successful venture.

Leadership Lesson #3 Learned:

Understanding the written and unwritten rules in any endeavor can keep you out of trouble and even save you strokes. What kind of person are you when it comes to playing by the rules? Does someone have to be watching over your shoulder to keep you honest? While most people will never say anything to your face, you can be sure they have you pegged by the third hole. They know what kind of person you are and how far you can be trusted. Can you live with that judgment? The genuine leader can and does.

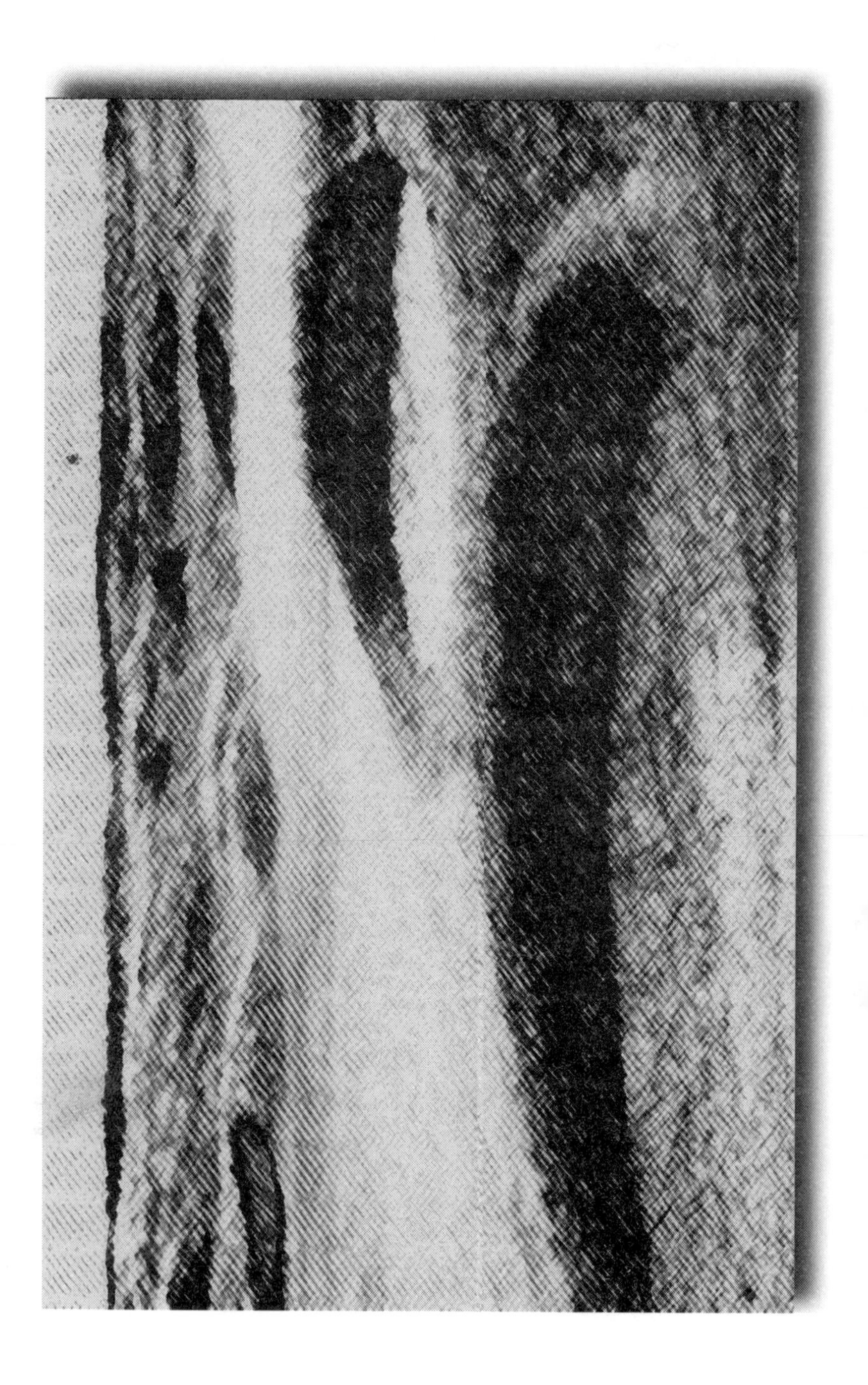

Leadership Lesson #4:
YOUR SWING BELONGS TO YOU

The leader learns that his swing belongs to him and only he can change it.

Leaders have their own unique style and form. One size does not fit all. A very important ingredient to being a successful leader is to discover your style, refine it, and be known for it.

There are as many different golf swings as there are leadership styles. Every golfer has his or her very own unique swing and style. From Arnold Palmer to Annika Sorenstam and Babe Deidricksen to Happy Gilmore – each golfer's swing is uniquely different, and yet, successful. The same is true of leaders.

Consider the leadership styles of two successful CEOs, Jack Welch and Scott McNealy, who are good golfers as well. Each has distinguished himself through his track record of accomplishments and business performance; and yet, their leadership methods and techniques are quite different. GE's Welch built his sterling reputation by transforming an already successful company. He took GE from a sleepy, but successful, conglomerate into a world-class business that in 1997 and 1998 ranked first in the world for net worth. He describes his leadership style as that of a "coach and passionate cheerleader." He challenges his managers to transform themselves into leaders who can inspire and empower their employees to get the job done.

Sun Microsystem's McNealy embraces a different approach; and yet, he is also very successful. McNealy describes himself as a non-techie who thrives on competition and likes to stay focused on his company's strategic direction. He's a marketing wizard and visionary who stimulates the creative energies of his employees and then weaves their best ideas into value-added products and services.

The analogies between golfers and leaders are profound because the game of golf and leadership share at least five similar cornerstones. Jack referred to these cornerstones as "The Five P's." They are Purpose, Principles, People, Processes, and Performance. According to Jack, everything we do in life, personally and professionally, can be categorized under one or more of The Five P's. He also taught me that The Five P's were relevant to the game of golf because championships were won by golfers who mastered their application in any given tournament.

Recently, I had the opportunity to reflect on this insight when I rediscovered my slice while playing a round of golf at Mt. Woodson Country Club near San Diego. For anyone who has played this challenging mountain course, it is an unforgiving environment when it comes to slices and shanks. It was a very frustrating back nine. I hadn't been plagued by my slice for several years but now it had come back to haunt me on the tight fairways of Mt. Woodson. And, just when I was gaining confidence in my irons. Curses! Hadn't I learned anything?

"So far as the golf swing is concerned in order to keep any part of it in perspective we must review the action as a whole. For, it is at its best, an unbroken motion. To stress one part unduly must destroy the rhythmic flow."

–Eric M. Prain
Live Hands

I immediately retreated to a practice range where I could examine my golf swing. Unfortunately, I couldn't seem to find the cause nor the cure. I went home tired and dejected. I plopped down on the living room sofa and rubbed my eyes. I noticed *Distance to the Green* on the coffee table. I opened it to the chapter on the golf swing and began to read about fear and risk; how to break bad habits, and apathy. What Gary Abram and Bob O'Byrne wrote was very helpful and got me thinking about the five stages of a golf swing.

Next, I picked up a copy of Ben Hogan's classic book, *The Modern Fundamentals of Golf* (Simon & Schuster) on the golf swing. It was there that I found the answer once I let go of my anger and frustration and paused long enough to reflect on what I was doing right, and more importantly, what I was doing wrong. I grabbed a 5 iron from my golf bag and stepped into my backyard. I started hitting practice balls into a driving net. I systematically began to re-examine my grip, stance, takeaway, downswing, and follow-through.

Next, I sought the advice of a golf instructor who reminded me of something I already knew but I wasn't applying. He told me to drop my right foot back two feet to force my hips to rotate. It was awkward at first, but I repeated this sequence ten times without striking a ball. I visualized in slow motion my complete swing and saw the ball landing down the middle of the fairway at the 150 yard marker. Only then, when that vision was fixed in my mind, did I tee-up a ball and repeat the same memory motions. Bingo! I hit the ball as straight as an arrow. Every now and then my slice reappears. But I know what causes that result, and when I don't like the outcome, I can change it. Now, I choose *not* to accept bad outcomes.

The successful leader must take time to reflect on his approach to managing people and problems. Sometimes we use the wrong tactic and get poor results. Every situation requires a different strategy just as every golf shot requires a slight modification in how we hit the ball; because no two shots are the same. But, according to the great teachers, your swing routine should never change. The same holds true for leaders. Every situation and every problem requires a slightly different response, but your approach should be consistent. Don't be the kind of golfer who attends the annual company golf tournament with the same flawed swing that he brought with him last year, and the year before that, and the year before that, too! Your colleagues want to see some progress in your ability to do a job – on and off the golf course.

Leadership Lesson #4 Learned:

A leader recognizes his swing is both a blessing and a curse. Just because you have a slice or hook, doesn't mean you're stuck with it. While your swing belongs to you, there is no reason it should remain flawed. Find a coach; someone who will observe your swing and help you correct the flaws and imperfections. In business, the successful leaders apply The Five P's to their everyday routine just as the professional golfer never stops practicing the five stages of a golf swing in his search for perfection.

Leadership Lesson #5:
TAKING LESSONS FROM A PRO

A leader knows that in order to improve his score, he must improve his game.

I have taken many golf lessons and each lesson taught me something valuable about my game. In fact, every lesson has improved my ability to play the game although it did not necessarily improve my score. Therein lies the ultimate lesson.

A golf pro can teach you technique and style and how to think through your shots. He can even help you correct your swing flaw. But only you can improve your score. That is up to you because you are solely responsible for how you swing and hit the ball. It's a matter of doing the right things right.

This is also why leaders spend time and money on executive coaches, physical fitness trainers, management consultants, and other professionals who have the ability to help them master their game.

"There are three ways of learning golf: by study, which is the most wearisome; by imitation, which is the most fallacious; and by experience, which is the most bitter."
–Robert Browning

Despite all the articles, magazines, and self-help books – including this one – only you can improve your score. And the best way to improve your score is by playing the game. That's why I believe that on-the-job training is the fastest and most effective way to learn and grow.

What Jack Rudabee taught me about taking lessons from a golf pro is this – Life is a process of continuous learning. By learning we can improve our results. If you aspire to be a better leader or golfer, then you must be committed to lifelong learning. This is why serious professionals take lessons. As the adage goes, "School is never out for the pro."

A golf instructor provides you with a mirror to see yourself in motion. When instructors first started using video cameras on the driving range to record their students' swings, I was fascinated. For the first time, I actually saw – not visualized – what the golf pro was trying to tell me about my outside-in swing pattern and how I was coming over the top of the ball on my downswing. I saw my right elbow fly open and my shoulder dip as I hit

"The player may experiment about his swing, his grip, his stance. It is only when he begins asking his caddie's advice that he is getting on dangerous ground."
–Sir Walter Simpson

"According to the USGA, only 8 percent of golfers in America take lessons from a teaching pro. Perhaps this is why so many golfers play poorly and never break 100."
–Tom Hinton

the ball. Thanks to the use of video, I can now see my mistakes and correct them. For the first time, my mind had a clear picture of why I was slicing and shanking the ball and what was producing that outcome. It was a real eye-opener for me.

The leader takes lessons to improve himself. He knows that in order to attain wisdom and success, he must find innovative and fun ways to inspire, challenge, and motivate his people. This requires us to embrace new ideas and let go of old habits and traditions that don't work as well anymore. It does no good to take lessons and then revert to old habits. The problem – both on the golf course and in business – is that people are too comfortable with what they know and how they presently do things. I refer to this comfort level as "the velvet rut." One word of caution here – even though a leader may have figured out a new way to build a better mousetrap, some people will spend more time and energy conjuring up reasons why it won't work instead of trying the new mousetrap. So, be persistent and relentless in pursuit of your goals. It's up to the leader to paint a video-clear picture of what the possibilities are for the future.

Ray Kroc, the venerable founder of McDonald's, said, "People are like bananas. They're either green and ripening, or yellow and rotting." He was referring not to the human appetite for Big Macs and tasty french fries, but rather, continuous learning. Perhaps this is why his company created Hamburger University, a place where employees learn about the art of perfecting fast food service according to McDonald's success formula.

Finally, it's important to seek the advice, wisdom, and counsel of others, provided they are committed to helping you achieve your goals. Too often we ask the advice of people, even loved ones, who are more concerned about how your decision will affect them than they are about helping you achieve your dreams.

Leadership Lesson #5 Learned:

Progressive leaders hire experts and coaches to help them develop their talents. They understand the importance of taking lessons from a pro. Their commitment to lifelong learning continues long after they've earned their college degree. Leaders also develop close relationships with a small group of confidants to ensure they maintain their equilibrium when making tough decisions.

Leadership Lesson #6:

BE THE BALL: HOW TO DEVELOP YOUR PROBLEM-SOLVING ABILITIES FROM THE INSIDE OUT

The leader has the ability to solve problems by thinking through the solution.

The genuine leader has the ability to solve problems by thinking through the solution. The ego-driven leader typically relies on fixing the blame before he fixes the problem. As you can imagine, most people in business who use this approach don't make many friends and, eventually, they are isolated and abandoned.

In golf, we say "be the ball." The disciplined golfer thinks about the solution by analyzing his challenge. The challenge in golf, of course, is getting the ball from the tee to the cup with the fewest number of strokes. When you observe a touring professional, you'll see the power of concentration at work. The pro learns early on in his career to block out the interference and "be the ball." The only way a golfer can mentally rehearse his swing routine is to "be the ball."

"To control his own ball, all alone without help or hindrance, the golfer must first and last entirely control himself, and himself only. The little round toy sitting so alone and so still, which has so fascinated and tantalized human beings for more than five centuries, is thus uniquely a psychic as well as physical cynosure of muscular skills and mental concentration."
–John Stuart Martin

A leader must also have the ability to concentrate on solving a problem by immersing himself in finding the right answer. When the leader analyzes the problem with the end purpose in mind, he sees things more clearly. Innovative possibilities begin to emerge.

The next time you are faced with a difficult challenge – on or off the golf course – try to "be the ball." Ask yourself these questions.

- What is my desired outcome?
- What is my process with regard to solving this problem or challenge?
- At what point will I know I have the right answer?
- How can I measure my process to ensure my results will work?
- How will I feel after solving this problem? Describe the solution in vivid, colorful words so your mind can absorb the mental picture you are creating.
- What will be my reward for achieving my desired outcome?

Leadership Lesson #6 Learned:

Whenever you are faced with a serious challenge or problem, take a deep breath and allow yourself to "be the ball." View it from a fresh perspective. Control your initial emotional response. Don't allow hostile emotions to pollute your thinking and stifle your creativity. Avoid the traps of resistance, resentment, and revenge. Stimulate your imagination by thinking through a series of potential solutions. Begin with the most absurd and off-the-wall solutions you can imagine and then work backwards towards a realistic solution. This type of creative thinking actually frees your mind and, ultimately, allows you to create solutions that are realistic, meaningful, and work!

Leadership Lesson #7:

ADDRESSING THE BALL: REHEARSE YOUR SWING

The leader never performs without first rehearsing.

The best golfers have a routine for addressing the ball. Jack Rudabee referred to these pre-swing and fairway routines as processes. Although the process varies greatly from one golfer to the next, there are certain characteristics and steps that appear in every golfer's routine.

For example, the experienced golfer finds a level spot on the tee box for his ball. Once he sets the ball on the tee, he steps back to determine the line of flight where he wants to hit the ball. He selects a specific location on the fairway where he wants to land his ball. Next, he adjusts his grip and observes his swing path; and, while taking a practice swing, he gauges the wind factor. Finally, he mentally reviews all of these steps, and while his mind is clearly focused on the desired outcome, he swings.

"The golf swing is like a suitcase into which we are trying to pack one too many items!"
–John Updike

Jack Rudabee taught me how to address the ball during our first summer together. He would have me stand behind him on the driving range and observe him. He rarely deviated from the routine I described above. During the years I caddied for him, he perfected his pre-shot routine and followed it religiously. I watched his handicap drop from 12 to eight in those seven years. I believe he was a better player at age 60 than when I first met him.

Jack Rudabee defined processes as the methods by which people get things done. In business, as in golf, having a manageable, winning process is an important key to success. People and companies are at their best when they have a system in place that maximizes their abilities and talents. The best golfers have a process for everything – how they practice, their pre-swing routine, how they address the ball, and how they manage the course.

In business, your processes will determine the quality of your products and services. Process Management has become an important dimension of every successful business. Jack believed there are four aspects of every successful process. They are: **standards, measurements, innovations,** and **improvement**.

Jack Rudabee understood that a successful business must have standards of performance. He defined standards as the benchmark for excellence. In golf, a course's par rating of 72 is a standard. A golf course's slope rating is another standard.

"The golf swing is like sex. You can't be thinking about the mechanics of the act while you're performing."
–Dave Hill

Measurements are very important because they reveal how you're progressing. In golf, each stroke measures your performance. How far you drive a 3-wood or a 5-iron is another measurement.

Innovation is your ability to change and progress so that you can remain competitive. Innovation is essential to every business because it requires leaders to stay close to their customers and shift their thinking in order to meet changing customer expectations. Jack understood this fact. This is why he altered his home designs and never built the same model twice on the same block. "People always want something faster, better, and cheaper," he was fond of saying. He strove to be uniquely different through innovation. In golf, innovation might be found in a backhanded wedge shot when your ball is lying under a pine tree. Or, it might be using the hilly slope of the 16th green at Augusta National in order to sink a birdie putt. Innovation requires us to think outside the box and test our courage against the forces of conformity.

Finally, process is about improvements. Everything can be improved. Look at the evolution of the golf ball, for example. Today, Titleist makes 320 different versions of a golf ball. Each one is designed to do something slightly different. Titleist's commitment to continuous improvement is one reason it is recognized around the world as the market leader in golf balls.

"If you set up correctly there is a chance you'll hit a reasonably good shot even if you make a mediocre swing. If you set up incorrectly, you'll hit a lousy shot even if you make the greatest swing in the world."

–Jack Nicklaus
Golf My Way

Cadillac, a Malcolm Baldrige National Quality Award winner, isn't content to simply duplicate last year's popular models or be the first to hop on the sports utility vehicle bandwagon. Instead, Cadillac decided to design the very best product and then build it. Despite being a latecomer to the SUV marketplace, Cadillac's sales have soared due to its quality and raising the bar on its competitors. Cadillac tweaks and improves each new model because of its focus on customer satisfaction and its employees' commitment to performance excellence. As Motorola's former quality champion, Wini Schaeffer, once told me, "Good enough, isn't! You must constantly improve or be banished to mediocrity."

In business, you need to know how to address the ball. Perhaps the ball represents a strategic marketing issue for your company or altering a product's features in order to meet shifting customer expectations. If you simply show-up without first having rehearsed and pre-determined your desired outcome, your results probably will be less than satisfactory.

In order for a leader to create positive results, he must take time to prepare. The genuine leader must develop processes that work – first time, every time – because, rarely, do we get a second chance to get it right.

The leader understands that preparation time is essential in order to create the desired outcome.

Leadership Lesson #7 Learned:

In order to increase your success ratio, develop processes that breed success. Whether you're on the golf course or in the middle of an important company project, have a methodology or routine that works for you. Take extra care to thoroughly prepare and rehearse your approach so you create your desired outcome before you even walk into the boardroom or step onto the tee box.

Leadership Lesson #8:

FOCUS, FEELING, AND FOLLOW-THROUGH: DEVELOPING YOUR LEADERSHIP RHYTHM

The leader understands that no task can be completed without the follow-through.

The successful leader understands that in order to consistently hit great shots, it is a matter of three things – focus, feeling, and follow-through.

Jack Rudabee once told me that it was his experience in business and politics that there were too many "potential leaders," and not enough genuine leaders. This is also true when you compare great golfers to the rest of the pack. But why?

The great golfers have the ability to focus all of their energies on their present shot. They aren't worried about what-ifs and coulda, shoulda, woulda. This power of concentration requires letting go of all your past shots and not worrying about the next hole. All that matters is the here-and-now. I mentioned in a previous lesson how difficult it can be to stay focused on *this* shot.

Sometimes other golfers are talking. Or, the gallery is celebrating a competitor's superb stroke on a neighboring green. It's a real challenge to concentrate your mental powers on hitting the ball when people are walking behind you or practicing their swing in your field of vision.

Greg Norman said, "the most important thing on the golf course is executing that first shot. Then that shot is gone and your next shot is the most important shot."

Like the seasoned golf pro, the leader must remain focused on the problem-at-hand. Once the strategic plan is complete and you're implementing that plan, it's essential to stay focused on your goals and tasks. Whenever a leader becomes distracted, the business will suffer. Employees will receive mixed signals and, eventually, their efforts will be hampered by the leader's inability to concentrate on the tasks-at-hand.

The great golfer also has a "feel" for each shot. He understands an excellent shot can only happen when he makes the proper club selection, accurately measures the distance to the green, and blends just enough physical power with raw nerve to hit the ball squarely to the target.

The leader also has a *feel* for his business and industry. He is sensitive to the customers' wants and needs. The bigger his heart, the better he will be as a leader because leadership is the soul of a business. A leader who can feel the pulse of the marketplace and is sensitive to his own organization will make better decisions.

Follow-through is ultimately what delivers the ball to the target. My friend, Jon Toolson, gave me excellent advice when he said, "As you complete your practice swing, make sure the clubhead hits you across your shoulder blades!" Every time I take his advice, I achieve a better swing result. For a while it hurt! But now, I appreciate knowing I've completed my swing and maximized my power. Once that muscle reflex becomes a learned habit, I don't have to worry about hitting my back anymore. I follow-through naturally and stop just in the nick of time from hitting my shoulder blades.

In business, keeping score, measuring results, and following through on your words and promises are essential to long-term success. The best leaders know this and, quite simply, just do it. Like a muscle reflex, it becomes second nature to them.

Maximilien Roberspierre said that "A leader has two important characteristics. First, he is going somewhere; second, he is able to persuade other people to go with him." Michael Maslak, the CEO of North Island Financial Credit Union in San Diego, California, echoed a similar thought when he told me that "best-in-class organizations achieve that status as a result of two essential ingredients – dynamic leadership and a successful strategy that people will believe in and rally around." Maslak, who led his credit union to national prominence as a winner of the California Quality Awards™ program and Arthur Andersen's Best Practices Award, embraces the Focus, Feeling, Follow-through philosophy on-and-off the golf course. He noted that too many leaders are fragmented and lose their focus when their vision for the future is overshadowed by the crisis-of-the-day.

This is also true on the golf course. When we make a mistake and shank our shot, too often we get flustered and compound our mistake by missing the next shot as well. Instead, as Mike Maslak suggests, we should recover quickly by getting back on the fairway and re-focus our attention on the goal – making par for the round. "One bad shot," notes Maslak, "doesn't ruin a round. But, carrying the memory of that bad shot with you to the second, third, and fourth tee box just might spoil your day!"

"The correct hitting motion is one unbroken thrust from the beginning of the downswing to the end of the follow-through."
–Ben Hogan

This is why Jack Rudabee – after hitting a bad shot – would pause and take a deep breathe and release his negative energy. Yes, he was mad and disappointed in his poor performance. But, he was also smart enough and had enough presence of mind to know that by letting go of that negative image, he could recover and get back onto the fairway. The longer we hold onto the negative memory, the longer it haunts us.

Jack once quoted Cicero on this very subject after driving his tee shot into the woods at Columbia Country Club in Bethesda, Maryland, during a charity tournament. "If Cicero were here," he said smiling, "he would remind us that 'it is the character of a brave and resolute man not to be ruffled by adversity and not to desert his post'. I guess I'll hit a provisional!" And he did – right down the middle of the fairway. As I recall, Jack scratched out a par on that hole with a beautiful wedge shot that rolled across the green and plopped into the cup. That's focus!

Leadership Lesson #8 Learned:

The leader appreciates the importance of staying focused on his goals. Avoid business dealings for which you have no feel. Be sure to develop a "feel" for your customers and employees. They should know you well enough to want to work for you and help you achieve your goals. Finally, always complete the loop. Follow-through on projects and keep your key people posted on your decisions, priorities, and especially, what you're thinking. Sometimes, they can suggest ways that keep you out of life's sandtraps.

Leadership Lesson #9:
THE PERFECT SHOT

The leader strives for perfection in the workplace.

I remember one Saturday morning in mid-October when the bright orange and red autumn leaves littered the green fairways, Jack Rudabee told his foursome a story about a golfer named Andy. Jack had played golf with him in Florida when Andy hit a perfect shot, his first hole-in-one.

Andy was an average golfer with a 22 handicap. On the fourth hole, a par three, Andy hit a seven wood about 175 yards into the cup on the fly. It was a spectacular sight to behold. The ball arched high off the tee and traveled over the edge of the lake that guarded the approach to the green. The ball drew slightly to the left where it came into perfect alignment with the pin. It cleared a sandtrap bordering the green and struck the flagstick at the precise point where it protrudes from the hole. It plopped into the hole and sank to the bottom of the cup. Jack said it was the noisiest hole-in-one he had ever witnessed. The golfers could hear the ball all the way from the tee box as it spanked the pin, careened straight down, and rattled around in the cup.

"I've never come anywhere near perfection. There is always something left to improve.

–Ben Hogan

When Jack recounted the story to us, he said he still got goosebumps every time he thought about it. Andy could hardly believe his good luck. In fact, he wasn't convinced he had scored a hole-in-one until he jogged up to the green, bent over the hole, and saw his ball snuggled in the bottom of the cup. He even checked twice to make sure it was his golf ball.

A golfer is never quite the same after he hits a perfect shot. A special bond is formed between the golfer and the hole he's aced. In many ways, from that moment forward, the hole belongs to the lucky golfer who aced it. It's a magical feeling to play with a golfer who makes a perfect shot because everyone becomes a believer – they know it can happen again! "Maybe, this time, I'll be the lucky one," I tell myself.

One of the most powerful lessons to be learned from scoring a hole-in-one is that it serves as a reminder that anything we put our minds to can be accomplished. The leader believes that nothing is impossible because the "Greatest Deed" has

"You must have confidence in your ability to make the shot required. This comes from practice. It also comes easier after you've been in a few pressure situations and have learned to handle them. There is no substitute for experience; and, the more you learn to react properly under pressure, the better you'll be able to perform the next time."

–Byron Nelson
Shape Your Swing the Modern Way

already been achieved. That deed, according to author Wu Wei, was the creation of the universe. As Wu Wei wrote in his book, *I Ching Life*, "Once that deed was accomplished, everything else became possible." He adds, "What that means for us is that we can rise to greatness, that we can accomplish our goals, no matter how lofty, that we can be who we want and have want we want; that everything is within our reach."

Perfection on the links reminds us that we are part of something which is unique and special. We are one people, with one purpose, and one common dream – to achieve perfection during our lifetime. A hole-in-one gives us that sense of accomplishment.

In business, the leader's job is to create an environment for perfection by eliminating roadblocks that inhibit solutions-oriented thinking by employees. The leader champions innovation by ridding his organization of antiquated policies, procedures, and rules that undermine team spirit, unity, commitment, and success. This is what companies like The Ritz Carlton Hotels, Solectron, Microsoft, and Hewlett Packard are doing.

Finally, the leader inspires his or her employees to excel by establishing realistic performance standards and then giving people broad authority to discover their own path to success. In this way, employees typically outperform management's expectations and break through glass ceilings.

"When we become slaves to the card and pencil, we become inclined to regard as total losses those rounds in which our score mounts beyond our reasonable expectancy."

–Bobby Jones
Bobby Jones on Golf

Like the golfer who seeks a perfect shot, the leader must clear away the organizational clutter in order for his employees to do their jobs and achieve superior results.

Leadership Lesson #9 Learned:

The leader recognizes that pockets of perfection exist throughout his organization. Excellence happens everyday in a thousand small, but meaningful, ways. When you arrive at work tomorrow, wear a new pair of glasses — the glasses of the genuine leader. Ask yourself these questions, "How can I inspire perfection in the workplace today?" "What will I do today that will give me a sense of complete fulfillment?" Resolve not to leave work until you've experienced that sensation.

Leadership Lesson #10:
ACCEPTING DEFEAT WITH DIGNITY

The leader is gracious in defeat and humble in victory.

Like every human being, I've experienced both victory and defeat. While I prefer victory over defeat any day, losing offers an important lesson in life. In fact, I believe experiencing defeat is one of life's most important leadership-building lessons.

Defeat is humbling. It's a sobering experience. Defeat tests the true fabric of a leader. Why? Because, displaying decorum and pride in the face of defeat is much more difficult than smiling while hoisting the winner's claret jug.

Defeat requires the leader to control his deepest emotions. It also requires the leader to set aside the hurt and overcome his frustration and anger in order to congratulate the victor. This is extremely difficult for many people. The leader's conduct and decorum in his moment of defeat reveals more about him than all his victories combined.

"Golf is a test of temper, a trial of honor, a revealer of character."

–David Forgan
St. Andrews,
Scotland

The genuine leader, regardless of the outcome, is gracious in defeat and humble in victory. This is because he understands the ups and downs of life. Nobody wins all the time. Even the greatest names in golf suffer defeat. The most important lesson a leader should take away in times of defeat is that his or her performance just wasn't up to par. Sometimes it's that simple. Little else matters because it won't change the outcome. So, get on with your life and put those losing moments behind you. Move on to the next match. If it was a flaw in your swing or a breakdown in your mental game, rediscover the right way to do it and get back on the winning track.

As Jack Rudabee taught me, leaders never lose hope. In fact, there is one major difference between a leader and a loser. When the leader suffers a setback he is able to rebound. When the loser suffers a defeat, he doesn't get up off the canvas. He just lays there – stunned and dazed, unable to recover. The loser is down for the count. The late, great boxer, Archie Moore, was once asked how he won so many fights. He replied, "I always got up when I was knocked down at least one more time than my opponent did!"

"Every golfer can expect to have four bad shots a round. When you do, just put them out of your mind and move on."

–Walter Hagen

"It took me 17 years to get 3,000 hits in baseball. I did it in one afternoon on the golf course!"

–Hank Aaron
Atlanta Braves and Home Run King of Baseball

Napoleon Hill, who authored *Think and Grow Rich,* said it best. "A winner never quits and a quitter never wins." While every leader has suffered setbacks and defeats, he is never finished until he throws in the towel.

Leadership Lesson #10 Learned:

Part of the honor of playing in a match is congratulating (or being congratulated by) your worthy opponent. Take the time to pay tribute to your opponent – win or lose – just as you would want to be acknowledged. This is the ultimate test of the leader's courage. Never give up for the wrong reason. Most of our defeats in life come as a result of inexperience or miscalculations. In golf, as in business and life, we can attribute most of our defeats to specific actions that can be cured with a few lessons or by tweaking our course management skills. Don't become a victim of defeat. Resolve in your mind to learn from it, take corrective action, improve your performance, and ultimately win. But, win or lose, always be gracious to your opponent.

Leadership Lesson #11:
REPLACE YOUR DIVOTS

The leader replaces his divots so the course is in better condition than he found it.

Last year, I revisited Spyglass Golf Course in Pebble Beach, the most spectacular golf setting in the United States. Spyglass is a beautiful, but challenging course. Early in my round, on a par four hole, I blasted a powerful drive off the tee that positioned me perfectly for my approach shot to the green. I was elated.

But when I reached my ball, it was lying in a deep brown divot. Some ten feet away was the clump of sod that another golfer had shoveled out of the earth during an earlier swing. Obviously, the golfer who left that brown scar on the picturesque fairway at Spyglass wasn't thinking about me or anyone else that foggy morning. He simply struck his ball, cut an eight inch divot in the carpet-like fairway, and walked away to his next shot.

I was upset for two reasons. First, my ball rolled into a divot leaving me with fewer options for my second shot. But, secondly, its inauspicious placement distracted me

"Never wash your ball on the tee of a water hole."
–Mulligan's Laws

from fully celebrating my excellent drive. Now, I knew how the late Payne Stewart felt in 1998 when he drove his tee shot down the center of the Olympic Club's 17th fairway only to see it roll into a sandy divot. Stewart was so disturbed by the ill-fated shot, he lost his composure and eventually the 1998 U.S. Open. Fortunately, Payne Stewart overcame the disappointment of losing at the Olympic Club and rebounded at Pinehurst Number 2 to win the 1999 U.S. Open. What a great lesson Stewart gave us in comebacks and one's determination to succeed!

At that moment, I vowed to always replace my divots. I also vowed to repair as many ball marks on the green as I could without delaying the game or distracting other players.

Every leader encounters divots during his day. The question is "How do we react to a divot?" A leader recognizes that he is responsible for solving problems and, more importantly, anticipating problems before they happen.

Leaders don't create a mess or leave it for someone else to clean up. Leaders understand that

"Golf is a game of blows and weapons. In order that the game continue we must make amends for every single act of destruction. In a golf club, everyone knows the player who does not replace his divot. One can guess how he leads the rest of his life."

–Shivas Irons
Golf in the Kingdom
by Michael Murphy

part of their responsibility is the maintenance and attention to small details like repairing flawed products, improving customer service, and accepting responsibility when things go wrong. It's all part of their unwritten job description. It is also the right thing to do.

A leader isn't consumed with pointing fingers and fixing blame. Instead, the leader fixes the *problem* and keeps his team moving forward – always focused on the goal of paring the course and determined to achieve it.

Leadership Lesson #11 Learned:

As you walk down the hallways at work, observe the divots. I continue to be impressed by the employees of five star hotels who will stop and pick-up a piece of paper because they take pride in their work environment. Likewise, a leader doesn't direct his employees to pick-up the trash. He models the behavior by doing it himself in the presence of others. The leader leads by example. Leaders demonstrate their commitment to principles through their actions, more so than by their words.

Leadership Lesson #12: CHOOSE YOUR PARTNERS WELL

Throughout life we are confronted by choices and consequences; and for better or worse, we must live with the consequences of our decisions.

Golfer Tony Lema once suggested, "In choosing a partner, always pick an optimist." Jack Rudabee and I were more than partners on the golf course, we became soulmates. It was through Jack's mentoring that I gained confidence in making decisions and, more importantly, standing by those decisions once they were made. Jack was the eternal optimist.

Jack believed that the "people" factor in his Five P's Model was crucial to every leader's success because without people, no task would get done. For it is by, through, and with people that the leader performs and achieves results. Jack Rudabee believed it was exceptional people who distinguished a best-in-class organization from the competition. While any business can make a good product or deliver acceptable service, only those companies that inspire and motivate their people to exceed expectations will achieve a best-in-class reputation.

Jack told me the most important factor in playing tournament golf was to choose your partners well. He also said that choosing a partner was the most important decision a person could make in business and life. This one decision, he said, spelled success or failure for millions of small business owners, corporations, marriages, and political campaigns. He offered me three simple rules for choosing a partner well.

First, he cautioned me, "Know yourself." Know your strengths and weaknesses. This is a very difficult task because it requires us to face the mirror and confront our imperfections as well as our talents. But, by knowing ourselves, we are better able to choose a partner who neutralizes our weaknesses and compliments our strengths. This is why Jack believed in the axiom, "Opposites attract." I noticed that many of Jack's senior managers were his opposite in their personality styles and business acumen. Jack surrounded himself with people who enjoyed "debating the details and counting the coins in the piggy bank." However, he preferred the rush of making deals and using the force of his personality to win friends and influence people.

Jack's style on the golf course was no different. When it came to choosing his golfing partner, he always preferred someone who could stick their wedge shot on the pin from 100 yards away. That was his weakness and he wanted a golfing partner who could cover his short game.

Secondly, he advised me that when choosing a partner, find out in advance their weaknesses. Once you've identified their weaknesses and any other quirks, ask yourself this key question, "Now that I know the negative side of this person, can I

"By nature, men are nearly alike; by practice, they get to be wide apart."
–Confucius

"All golfers, men and women, professional and amateur, are united by one thing - their desire to improve.
–Judy Rankin

live with them as my partner in this venture?" If your gut reaction tells you "no way," then don't get hitched. This is one reason why Jack always wanted to play golf with a prospective client or senior manager before he contracted to work with them. Jack believed that a person's conduct, decorum, and integrity on the golf course was a mirror image of how they would conduct themselves on the job. If somebody cheated on the golf course or didn't adhere to the rules of the game, there was little chance they would act honorably in a business relationship.

Thirdly, Jack believed that a good partner always stood by his colleagues. When someone is feeling down, a true partner should be their biggest supporter and help raise their spirits. When they achieve success, the partner acts as a cheerleader to help them celebrate their accomplishments. Never be a drag on your partnership. Always be loyal and supportive. "If you follow these three simple rules," Jack told me, "you'll enjoy partners for life."

Leadership Lesson #12 Learned:

There are few things more important in life than choosing your partners well. This applies equally to golf, business, and marriage. In most cases, our intuitive sense will tell us the right answer. When it comes to love, let your heart decide. When it comes to business deals, financial matters, and golf, let your head make the partnering decision. Chances are, if you follow this strategy, you'll choose the right partner.

Leadership Lesson #13: WALKING THE COURSE

A leader always walks the course before he plays the game.

A few days ago, as I was standing in the Chicago O'Hare Airport concourse waiting for my flight to board, I looked out the windows onto the tarmac. I noticed two American Airline pilots inspecting their jet. They were meticulously examining every aspect of that plane to ensure it met their standards.

They reminded me of Jack Rudabee, who made a habit of walking an unfamiliar golf course before he played it. In his later years, when age and old war wounds took their toll, he resorted to driving a golf cart up and down the cart paths to better understand the lay of the land. Jack's purpose in walking the course was to prepare him for what laid ahead.

In business, Jack always "walked the course." For example, Jack never purchased an existing hotel until he had slept there and experienced the service, ambiance, and quality of the property and the staff. He never bought an empty lot or a building site without camping out there for 24 hours. His competitors teased him about doing this; they suggested it was a waste of time. But, Jack said it gave him innovative ideas on how to enhance the land's use. As a result of his "24-hour camp-outs," Jack gained valuable insights on how people lived and how his structure would compliment their social patterns and local customs. This insight supported Jack's mission to build "harmonious communities." It also helped him avoid lawsuits by well-intentioned community advocates.

In Scotland, golfers usually walk the course. Walking the course is healthy exercise and it is also considered the way the game should be played. By walking the course, Scots can study the curves of the fairways and the bends of each green. For the Scots, walking the course conditions them physically and mentally. This is why today most Scots still resist the temptation to use golf carts and instead rely on trolleys, caddies, or tote their own golf bag.

Jack believed the Scots understood the game of golf to be a process in which the journey was more important than the final score. He relished his annual trip to Scotland in mid-September where he played several courses along the Firth of Forth and in the historic town of St. Andrews. And, Jack appreciated the Scots ability to preserve the game of golf in its purest form. "In America," he fussed, "we have created an industry around the game. Equipment manufacturers, instructors, golf schools, driving ranges, golf carts, and product shows." Although Jack marveled at America's "Yankee Ingenuity" and our ability to "turn a buck," he preferred the Scottish version of golf because of its commitment to tradition and simplicity. "Golf," he remarked, "is a thinking

"Course Management is making the right choices. To do that you need to analyze the situation."

–Scott Simpson

man's game; it's like chess because it requires a player to think about his options before he makes his move. You can't just go out there and whack away at the ball. You must think about your lie, your shot, and how to make the right decision if you intend to score well on a golf course."

I think this is but one more reason why the Scots continue to walk their courses. It gives them time to think and reflect and enjoy the natural beauty of their surroundings. It also allows them to focus on the inner-dimension of the game and explore all the possibilities before they execute their shots.

In business, the prudent leader "walks the course." He knows that in order to help his employees better serve their customers, the leader must understand how customers do business, the processes they use, and their expectations. In this way, the leader stays connected to the real world and what's truly important to his employees. The authentic leader always walks his talk.

Leadership Lesson #13 Learned:

Don't allow yourself to be surprised by what's lurking around the bend. It is always better to take a few minutes to analyze a situation before you venture off into the unknown. Preparation is part of the answer to creating a successful outcome. So, take the time to "walk the course" of each and every venture you're about to enter so that you can better understand the potential opportunities as well as the traps that lie ahead. And take the time to stop and smell the roses and azaleas as you stroll down the fairways of life.

Leadership Lesson #14:

GAUGING THE WIND: THE LEADER ASKS "WHY?"

A leader understands it is more important to ask the right questions than to always have the right answers.

Several years ago, I made my first trip to Japan to address a Tokyo-based company on the subject of leadership. I was impressed by a Zen fable my Japanese hosts told me about a young man who had inherited a manufacturing business from his father. The young man was a capable manager of the business, but he had one very serious leadership flaw. He was impatient.

One day, the impatient young owner decided he needed to learn the game of golf in order to expand his circle of business friends. He was a gifted athlete, but he had never played golf. He scheduled a series of golf lessons with a Zen teacher. At their first lesson, no golf clubs were removed from the young man's golf bag; no practice shots were hit. Instead, the Zen teacher stood on the practice range with his pupil and asked him three questions:

First, the Zen teacher asked, "Why do you want to play this game?" The young owner replied, "To expand my business." Secondly, the Zen teacher asked, "How good do you want to be at this challenging game?" The young owner responded, "I am a talented athlete. I want to be the best player at my club." Then, the Zen teacher, wetted his right index finger and hoisted it to the sky to determine the direction and strength of the wind.

He asked the young manager, "I wonder how strong the wind is today?" The young man curtly replied, "What difference does it make. Let's get on with the lesson." The Zen teacher said calmly to his student, "Go home. I cannot teach you what you refuse to learn." Stunned by the harshness of the Zen teacher's words, the young man pleaded with his instructor to teach him the game. But, the Zen teacher continued to walk away as he gauged the strength of the wind by wetting his index finger again and raising it in the air.

The lesson the Zen teacher was trying to teach the impatient student relates to the "why?" question. The young manager had no interest in the game of golf. He simply wanted to be around potential clients. The Zen teacher wasn't satisfied with that response because he knew he could not teach the young man about a game for which he had no genuine interest. The student would have embarrassed himself – and his Zen teacher – on the golf course. The embarrassment would not have been due to poor play necessarily; but rather, due to a lack of consideration for the

"The superior man wishes to be slow in his speech and earnest in his conduct."
–Confucius

"The instant that your sense of feel is lost or becomes disconnected, your swing becomes disconnected also, and your power evaporates into thin air, like the sparkle from champagne when the cork is left out."

–Percy Boomer
On Learning Golf

play of others, the rules of the game, and disrespect for an ancient tradition which has evolved over six centuries.

Knowing "why" people are motivated to do certain things is paramount also to understanding what drives people towards success or drags them down. The authentic leader understands that by asking "why" questions he improves his odds for success.

Jack Rudabee would have appreciated this story because he enjoyed asking "why?" questions. He knew that by repeatedly asking people the "why?" question they would be challenged to think; and, eventually, when people are challenged to think they usually arrive at a better answer or solution to their problem. By asking people the "why?" question, Jack avoided costly errors and reduced the number of mistakes attributed to impatience and poor judgment.

An impatient manager, like the young man who refused to learn the lesson from his Zen golf teacher, expects immediate results without going through all the necessary preparation. This style of leadership is referred to as "ready, fire, aim!" In most cases it doesn't work because it omits a very crucial step – asking the "why" questions. A manager who fails to ask "why?" questions typically makes

"For a man to conquer himself is the first and noblest of all victories."
–Plato

snap decisions based on erroneous facts and faulty or incomplete data.

Another important reason to ask the "why?" question is this: over time conditions change. Dr. Albert Einstein understood this lesson better than most people and he exhibited his superior knowledge one spring morning during a final exam. A student approached the distinguished professor shortly after Dr. Einstein had distributed the test questions. The student said, " Dr. Einstein, do you realize these are the same test questions you gave us last semester?" Unperturbed, Dr. Einstein looked up from his desk and whimsically replied, "Ah yes, but since then the answers have changed!"

Leadership Lesson #14 Learned:

Sometimes the most profound questions to ask are the simplest. Questions are a non-threatening way to force people to think about what they are doing and the results they can expect. Asking questions is an excellent way to hold people accountable for their actions. If your people know you are going to ask "why" and "how" questions, they will re-double their efforts to get it right the first time. Build your reputation as a leader who raises his finger to the wind and asks simple, but penetrating questions like "why?" and "how?" This is the foundation for every successful process. And, as the Zen masters have taught us, never try to teach a pig to sing because it irritates the pig and frustrates everyone involved in the process.

Leadership Lesson #15:
LINE UP YOUR PUTTS

A leader understands that very few putts travel straight to the cup.

One dreary humid August morning on the golf course, as Jack Rudabee was waiting his turn to line up a five-foot putt on the 12th hole, he told his insurance agent a brief story about how he had saved his construction company over a million dollars by "paying attention to the details."

A few weeks earlier, Jack drove out to a new housing construction site in Gaithersburg, Maryland. It was a development of 250 upscale homes that Jack's company was building. A subcontractor had just completed installing the flashing paper below the window frames on three model homes. The crew was new on the job and, apparently their foreman left early to go fishing without inspecting the quality of the finished work. When Jack arrived, he quietly made his own inspection to ensure things were done according to his standards. He happened to notice the improper installation. Had

"Reading a green is like reading the small type of a contract. If you don't read it with painstaking care, you are likely to be in trouble."
–Claude Hamilton

the problem gone undetected, severe water damage could have occurred in all the new homes. This error could have cost Jack and his insurance company nearly a million dollars to repair.

Jack brought the matter to his superintendent's attention, who had the subcontractor repair the work and retrain his crew on how to install the flashing paper correctly.

Jack added, "Lining up a putt is no different than building houses or designing information systems. It's all in the details and the processes you use to get the job done right *the first time*.

You must think through your processes and stay focused on the result – putting the ball into the cup. If you deviate from a structured thought process, you will almost certainly miss the cup." Golfer Bob Rosburg once said, "To sink the ball in the hole, you must *think* the ball in the hole."

On the subject of making five-foot putts, Bobby Jones once remarked, "If it was easy, anyone could do it." Human beings are imperfect creatures. This is why creating a successful process that yields increased results is so difficult.

"Golf is really three games in one - the drive, the approach, and the putt. Ability in any one of the three departments does not necessarily carry with it skill in the other two. It is the coordination of all three at once, at the same time, that spells success."

–Walter J. Travis
Building Up Your Game

"If you look upon putting with fear and trembling, well then, the pixies that dance about the greens will turn your ball to one side or another when it is going straight for the hole."

–Andra Kirkaldy
Fifty Years of Golf: My Memories

At the same time, however, Jack believed that gut feeling or "intuition" was a big part of any successful process. "You must have confidence that your process will work," he argued, "and being right builds a person's confidence."

Perhaps the greatest lesson I've witnessed when it comes to building one's confidence and lining up the putt, was Bob May's amazing stroke on the 18th hole of Valhalla during the 2000 PGA Championship. May had to make his putt to force a playoff with defending champ, Tiger Woods. The golf world was transfixed as Bob May's putt snaked its way from the fringe of the green into the cup 12 feet away!

Leadership Lesson #15 Learned:

Making the right decision is like making a 12-foot putt. You had better think through all the possibilities and anticipate what will happen if your ball moves left or right along the way. Once you've done the prep work and developed a well-conceived process, striking the ball is the easy part. It's lining up your putt and visualizing all the possibilities that's the difficult part. This is why more golfers miss "gimme" putts than make them.

Leadership Lesson #16:
CELEBRATE OTHERS' SUCCESSES

A leader enjoys celebrating the success of others, especially a worthy opponent.

Harvey Penick said it best, "Be brave if you lose and meek if you win." One of the greatest attributes of golf is a player's ability to humble himself long enough to congratulate a worthy opponent on his success. As previously discussed in Leadership Lesson #10, after the game is over, it is not only good sportsmanship to congratulate your opponent, but to offer that congratulations with sincerity.

This does not imply that we must surrender our pride or stop rooting for ourselves. Arnold Palmer said, "I never rooted against an opponent, but I never rooted for one either!" This is why, in business and in golf, it is both fitting and proper for us to compliment our opponent when they make a great shot, win the match, or land a competitive business deal at our expense.

"You win by working, by concentration and desire. The key is preparation. You have to be prepared."

–Patty Berg
The Links Letter

I've watched many televised golf events and walked hundreds of fairways at various PGA and LPGA tournaments. I have always been impressed by the courage and character golfers display when their opponent makes a remarkable shot to win the event. It is not uncommon to see a slight smile and a tip of the hat from one's opponent. Most recently, I witnessed David Duval's remarkable final round performance at the Bob Hope Classic in Palm Springs where he blitzed the field with a record-tying score of 59!

His competitors were both awed and genuinely impressed by his performance including an Eagle on the 18th hole. And, they showed it with high fives and genuine smiles of congratulations.

These gestures are based on respect and common courtesy. It is one of the great hallmarks of golf. Regrettably, I don't see enough players in other professional sports extending a helping hand to lift an opponent to his feet after he's been knocked down; or applaud an outstanding play as Sammy Sosa did when Mark McGwire hit his 62nd home run. That's class!

"Golf is a game made up of errors. Learning to cope with feelings or failure and imperfections is one of the keys to freeing the mind and allowing yourself to play to the best of your ability."
–Vivien Saunders
The Golfing Mind

"Do not gloat when your enemy falls; when he stumbles, do not let your heart rejoice."
–Proverbs 24:17

This lesson is a powerful one because it reminds us that winning is a reflection of one's courage and respect for people. It is also a sign of maturity. One day you're on top of the world; the next day you're struggling to stand. A leader must be strong enough to withstand the shell-shock of victory or defeat. But, in the course of playing the game, the leader must know how to celebrate an opponent's success. Why? Because, the cup of success is plentiful and it will never go dry.

What I have learned from golf is that there is abundance in the world; enough for everyone to experience success and enjoy a fulfilling life. It makes no sense that our Creator would place us on this planet without everything we need to succeed and enjoy a prosperous life.

The higher ground is to learn this powerful leadership lesson and apply it in our business dealings. The leader is able to share in the good fortune of another's accomplishments even when he desperately wants to win.

The enlightened leader recognizes that we live in a world of abundance – there is more than enough for those who focus on their goals and capitalize on the many opportunities offered us. "It is not a question of hard work because what we love to do should not be considered 'hard work.'" The fact is we enjoy what we do so much that we would do it for free; however, we are good enough that someone is willing to pay us to do it!

So, when you find yourself one stroke down and the match is lost, take a page from PGA member Bob May. Give your worthy competitor his due credit for outscoring you. Sometimes, second place is your best place.

The next time a worthy opponent edges out your company in a hard-fought struggle for a contract or business venture, send them a heartfelt congratulatory note in the spirit of true gamesmanship. Let them know that you genuinely wish their company and employees every success because you would want the same for yourself and your people. This positive approach "raises the bar" and provides you with a much-deserved "opportunity for humility." I guarantee it will knock your competitor's socks off. They'll never expect it; and so, it gives you the higher ground. This will help you grow as a leader and help re-focus your efforts on winning the next time around. It also will move you quickly out of a negative frame of mind and into a positive, get-on-with-the-game attitude.

Leadership Lesson #16 Learned:

Make two resolutions today. First resolve that you will celebrate another person's success by attending or organizing a celebration in your company in the next ten days. Show your leadership colors by celebrating the accomplishments of someone in your organization who has given much and contributed to your company's success. By the way, the lower on the totem pole that person is, the greater the impact your presence will have throughout the organization.

Secondly, resolve to congratulate a competitor for a job well done. Check your ego at the door and make the decision to telephone your congratulations, or send flowers. As long as your ego is in the way, you will never be able to experience the true satisfaction that accompanies success. Celebrate the success of others and grow from it.

Leadership Lesson #17:
LUCKY BREAKS AND MEMBER BOUNCES

The leader creates his own luck.

A winning performance requires many things, but especially skill and persistence. And, every now and then, a championship performance also requires a lucky break or a "member bounce."

Performance ultimately boils down to the number we write in that little box on the scorecard. There is no reason to make the score box any larger because the number in it says it all. It requires no detailed explanation, no complex interpretation, no flimsy excuses – the number in the box *is* the story.

For certain people, this is a disturbing fact. They have a need to supplement their score in business and life with footnotes, anecdotes, and parenthetical reasons as to why things happened the way they did. But, the fact is no explanation – no matter how eloquent or comprehensive – will change the outcome. The number in that small score box doesn't change.

Author and speaker Brian Klemmer reminds me, "Facts are friendly; always fair, but sometimes harsh." As much as we'd like to change certain facts – like our score of 10 on a par 5 hole, we can't do so without being dishonest. The good news is that tomorrow brings yet another day and one more opportunity to improve your performance.

Finally, performance is linked to your legacy. How do you want to be remembered? The leader recognizes that the ultimate test is to build one's legacy on the basis of how much he loved, how much he lived, and how much he learned and passed on to others. Legacy is also a measure of your significance on this earth. When your life is exhausted, will you leave a vacancy on this planet? Will your spirit be missed?

Jack Rudabee believed a leader creates his own luck. In order to transform lemons into lemonade, a leader must constantly reshape his physical and mental environment to create positive outcomes. This is how a leader is able to cause good fortune to start rolling his way. This transformation is created by combining three of the "18 Leadership Attributes" which I shared with you in the beginning of this book. The three leadership attributes necessary to create more lucky breaks and member bounces are **Focus and Determination, Self-Confidence**, and **Physical/Emotional Stamina**.

At the 1997 Masters Tournament, Tiger Woods captivated the world with one of the greatest displays of championship golf in the 20th century. Tiger Woods didn't rely on celestial powers or poor play by his competitors to win The Masters. He created his own luck by never three-putting a green and minimizing mental mistakes that could have cost him strokes. He remained focused on his goal and did not allow a few errant shots during his opening round to undermine his self-confidence or game plan.

He combined those three leadership attributes with his own natural talent to create several member bounces and a truly unforgettable performance.

"The fundamental problem with golf is that every so often, no matter how lacking you may be in the essential virtues required of a steady player, the odds are that one day you will hit the ball straight, hard, and out of sight. This is the essential frustration of this excruciating sport. For, when you've done it once, you make the fundamental error of asking yourself why you can't do it all the time. The answer to this question is simple: the first time was a fluke!"
–Colin Bowles

"Golf is a game that requires us to accept imperfection. Anyone who plays golf must realize that the perfect game has never been played. It never will be played or ever could be played."
–Harry Vardon

His poise, along with a clear sense of focus and self-confidence, gave Tiger the physical and emotional stamina necessary to play a superb final round and win by a record-breaking total score of 270 strokes, a 12-stroke margin of victory.

But Tiger wasn't content with his performance. He would rather be good than lucky. This is why he set out to refine his swing and improve his game. The results were clearly evident at the 100th U.S. Open at Pebble Beach where Tiger outshot the competition by an amazing 15 strokes. Sure, he had a few lucky breaks and member bounces – but a championship performance was at the root of his success.

Not to rest on his awe-inspiring U.S. Open victory at Pebble Beach, Tiger Woods completed the Grand Slam of Golf with an equally dominating win at the British Open on the Old Course at St. Andrews.

His 19-under par total of 269 strokes broke the major championship record for low score at the British Open. At age 24, Tiger is the youngest player to ever achieve the Grand Slam which requires a golfer to win the U.S. Open, the PGA Championship, The Masters, and the British Open. What's even more amazing is that only four golfers have achieved this mark of excellence. Tiger Woods' name will forever be joined with the elite company of Jack Nicklaus, Gene Sarazen, Ben Hogan, and Gary Player.

Tiger's victories at The Masters and the U.S. Open are excellent examples of what Jack Rudabee meant when he told me the leader creates his own luck. Jack believed the golf ball is an extension of the golfer which, reacts to the karma of the player. Positive energy begets positive bounces and favorable rolls. For example, how many times have you been "on a roll" and had your golf ball bounce off a rock or smack a tree and land in the middle of the fairway? Is this simply a coincidence or did your karma steer it back into play? Jack believed people possess the power to cause certain outcomes – favorable or unfavorable – through their power of concentration.

Golf highlight videos will forever remind us of lucky breaks and member bounces such as Sergio Garcia's miraculous "close-your-eyes and swing at the stump of the tree" shot during the 1999 PGA Championship at Medinah. But Sergio also created his own luck through his determination and planning. Some will say Tiger Woods got lucky at Valhalla during The 2000 PGA Championship, which he won when challenger Bob May faultered during the three-hole playoff. But, again, champions seize the opportunity by making the vital shots and capitalizing on a competitor's errors.

Perhaps this explains why only a few individuals in every profession achieve outstanding success, while most of their colleagues struggle on the fairways of life and business. Successful people know how to harness positive energy and use their power of concentration to create a positive outcome. The end result is they make their own luck and, in the process, get many more member bounces than the rest of the pack. And, so can you! As professional golfer Don January once advised, "Hit the ball; and when you find it, hit it again." Don't be surprised to find your ball exactly where you hoped it would be when you combine those three powerful leadership attributes and raise your goals and self-expectations to achieve a better performance.

Leadership Lesson #17 Learned:

Earl Nightengale suggested that "We become what we think about." Each of us can create a winning performance by thinking through our desired results. The leader enjoys more "member bounces" not because he has fewer problems or challenges, but because he is constantly thinking about how to achieve positive outcomes. He always thinks about the 300 yard drive instead of just getting the ball over the lake.

Leadership Lesson #18: PLAY TO YOUR OWN PAR

A leader understands that everyone has a handicap. It's nature's way of leveling the playing field of life.

The last time I was with Jack Rudabee on a golf course, he reminded me that there are two kinds of pars. The first par is the official stroke count listed on the score card. It varies from course to course, but typically a golf course will have a par of 72. The second kind of par takes into consideration a player's handicap. "Everyone," Jack noted, "has the benefit of a handicap on the golf course as well as in life." On the subject of handicaps, Jack once played golf with President Lyndon Johnson who told him, "I don't have a handicap. I'm *all* handicap!" Even world leaders are humbled on the links.

Golf is a sport that is based on fairness. This is why in golf, a better golfer must give strokes to a player of lesser ability. A handicap is a very positive thing because it levels the playing field and gives everybody a fair chance. "It's gamesmanship at its best," Jack exclaimed. "A handicap system," he noted, "allows everybody to play to their own par."

"We define 'handicap' as follows: an allocation of strokes on one or more holes that permits two golfers of very different ability to do equally poorly on the same course."

–Henry Beard and Roy McKie

This is why golf is as much an intellectual game as it is a test of physical endurance. Arnold Palmer accurately expressed it when he said, "Golf is deceptively simple, yet endlessly complicated." By the very rules of the game, we are given a unique opportunity through the handicap system to beat someone of greater ability and, hopefully, lower our own score.

The challenge we face as golfers and leaders is to always try to reduce our handicap. We constantly struggle with two opposing concepts in terms of our handicap – the benefit of receiving strokes to balance our score against superior players;

and, lowering our handicap in order to win on our own merit. It is the yin and yang of life. It is easier said than done because no two courses are the same.

Jack Rudabee trusted the handicap system. This is why he never offered advice nor counseled a player during their game. On the subject of giving advice, Jack followed British writer P.G. Wodehouse's counsel which was, "I always advise people never to give advice." Jack refrained from stepping in and offering corrective advice even when asked. He refused to become a coach on the golf course. His standard reply to any coaching question was, "I'd suggest you ask a teaching pro."

It wasn't that he didn't want to help another player improve his game; rather he didn't feel he was a trained professional who could accurately analyze someone's swing. And he certainly didn't want to mess with someone's mind in the middle of their round. Also, he didn't want to break the rules which limit players from giving advice during a game.

Jack believed in a very basic principle that, if followed, would allow people to achieve a winning performance in life. That principle was simply this: everyone needs to play to his or her own par. Each of us has different

> "You win by working, by concentration and desire. The key is I've always believed that golfers need to know their own game, what they're capable of doing and what they're not. Know these things so you can formulate a game plan and make good decisions for each course and each round."
>
> –Tom Lehman
> Live Hands

talents and abilities. This is part of our uniqueness and individuality. We are dealt different hands in life. But each of us is given a *handicap* that levels the playing field. This is a positive thing. Your *handicap* may come in the form of talents, energy, family, money, or some other gift that allows you to succeed in life. This is why the better golfers must give strokes to those with less talent as defined by their registered handicap. This is why the handicap system was created – to ensure fairness and an equal opportunity for all on the golf links.

In life and business, the leader appreciates that everyone has certain talents and abilities. The leader's primary job is to discover those talents and put them to work in an effort to improve both an employee's performance and results.

At the same time, no one is perfect. This is why players can't walk on water and presidents can't always fix what's broken in a company or a nation. And nature ensures it stays that way – in every game, in every industry, in every generation. Golf, like life, is a challenge. But it is fair; often harsh, but always fair. This is why no one ever walks away with *all* the skins *all* the time.

Leadership Lesson #18 Learned:

In order to play to your own par, you must determine your handicap. Perform a self-assessment. Ask yourself three important questions. What are my strengths? What are my weaknesses? And, finally — given my strengths and weaknesses, what can I accomplish in the next week, month, or year that is significant?

Stop thinking you must beat your opponent's score and start playing against the real opponent, the golf course. In business, your opponent is the educated customer who is always looking for a way to get it faster, better, and less expensively.

Remind yourself that the primary purpose of a handicap is to give you a fair chance and make up for your imperfections on the golf course. And then, surprise yourself by playing better than your handicap allows. Each time you play golf, try to lower your score by making one less mistake and getting lucky at least once during the round. And, every time you serve a customer try to add just a pinch of spice – something memorable – that will keep him coming back for more!

The 19th Hole:
LEAVE A LASTING LEGACY

The worth of the leader can be summarized by four things: the quality of his life; how much he loved; what he learned and taught to others; and, his message. These four attributes create the leader's legacy.

Nearly a decade has passed since Jack Rudabee died. He was buried in Arlington National Cemetery on a sloping hillside looking eastward towards our Nation's capital. It is a fitting resting place for so many of our national heroes and legends because from this beautiful vantage point they can watch over our nation and those to whom they have entrusted our legacy of freedom and prosperity. Last year, I kept a personal promise to visit Jack's final resting place.

I arrived on a sunny October afternoon. The wind was still. I stood there looking out over the hillside dotted with rows of white crosses. I reflected on the many conversations Jack and I had shared and how his wisdom and counsel had guided me throughout my life. I remembered that Jack was a giver and that's how he would want to be remembered– as someone who made

"I'm glad to give something back to the game I love so much."
–Byron Nelson

a measurable difference during his lifetime not because he was financially successful, but because he was committed to achieving significant things for others during his life.

Near the neat rows of simple white crosses was a weathered bench. I sat there until the sun slipped behind the silent hills and reflected on the 72 leadership lessons Jack gave me. In my hand was that spiral-bound notebook where I had stored his wisdom for all these years. As I read through it one more time, I recalled what Jack told me about a person's legacy. It was determined by four factors: how much you lived; how much you loved; what you learned; and, what you gave to others.

I remembered a story Jack once told me about legacies and how our lives do make a difference. The story was told to him by Eknath Easwaran, a student of Mahatma Gandhi and founder of the Blue Mountain Center of Meditation in Petaluma, California.

In 1947, a young British journalist was asked by his London newspaper to travel to India and interview Mahatma Gandhi. The exhausting journey took more than a week. Finally, the young reporter arrived at a small village in the southern province of India where he saw Gandhi boarding a train

IT IS NOT WHAT WE TAKE UP, BUT WHAT WE GIVE UP THAT MAKES US RICH."

–HENRY WARD BEECHER

to carry him to his next stop. The reporter, not wanting to miss his opportunity to interview Gandhi, leaped from his open car and ran along the train tracks until he reached the slow-moving train carrying Gandhi. The reporter shouted out a question to Gandhi who sat peacefully by an open window, "Do you have a message I can take back to the people of Great Britain?" Without speaking, Gandhi picked up a pen and a sheet of paper and scribbled a few words. He held the paper up to the window for the reporter to read. Gandhi had written, "My life is my message."

Jack believed that your passion in life is your message.

The principles, values, and beliefs you exhibit on the job, on the links, and at home are your message.

The thoughts you think are your message. The people you hire, associate with, and marry are your message.

The processes you use to perform your work, and the standards for excellence you establish, are your message.

> And the performance you give – whether it is a winning performance or your worst performance – that, too, is your message.
>
> And, ultimately, your message becomes your legacy.

As I went to close my tattered, water-stained notebook, I rediscovered a folded piece of paper hidden between the back pages. It was a prayer Jack Rudabee had given to me the last time we were together. Jack told me he entered each day by reciting it. It was written by the late Dr. Heartsill Wilson. I read it to myself once again.

A Prayer for Today

This is the beginning of a new day.
God has given me this day to use it as I will.
I can waste it or use it for good.
But what I do today is important because
I am exchanging a day of my life for it.

When tomorrow comes,
this day will be gone forever
leaving in its place
something I have traded for it.

I want it to be gain and not loss;
good, and not evil,
success, and not failure,
in order that I shall not regret the price
that I have paid for it.

About the Author:

Tom Hinton is a business author and professional speaker who lives in San Diego, California. Tom serves on the Board of Directors of the Leadership Links Foundation, a non-profit organization dedicated to teaching America's youth and business people about leadership through the game and principles of golf. Tom is also CEO of the Customer Relations Institute (CRI), an international training and consulting firm based in San Diego, California. He is the author of *The Spirit of Service*, and co-author of *Customer-Focused Quality: What to Do on Monday Morning*. Tom has addressed over 500 corporations, associations, and government agencies in the United States, Canada, Germany, Japan, England, Scotland and Mexico.

For information on Tom Hinton's speeches or training programs, you may contact him at Post Office Box 880774, San Diego, CA 92168-0774 or call CRI toll free at 1-800-544-0414. His e-mail address is tom@tomhinton.com.

SHARE YOUR LEADERSHIP LESSONS WITH TOM HINTON

Author Tom Hinton wants to hear from you! Share the Leadership Lessons You've Learned on the Links and he'll send you a special gift: a printed copy of the *18 Leadership Attributes* from Book One of this series. Send it to: **tom@tomhinton.com** or you can mail this page to: Tom Hinton c/o Blue Carriage Publishing, Post Office Box 880774, San Diego, CA 92168-0774.

My favorite Leadership Lesson I Learned on the Links is:

____
____
____
____
____
____
____
____
____
____
____
____
____
____
____

Your Name: ________________________________

Title: ________________________________

Company: ________________________________

Mailing Address: ________________________________

City: ______________ **State:** ______ **Zip:** _________

Email: ________________________________

Blue Carriage Publishing Company
Post Office Box 880774
San Diego, CA 92168-0774
www.bluecarriage.com

ORDER FORM

Bill to/Ship to: (No P.O. Boxes)

Name: ______________________

Address: ______________________

City: ______________________

State: ________ Postal/Zip: ______________________

Phone: ______________________

Fax: ______________________

E-Mail: ______________________

URL: ______________________

Delivery/Special Instructions: ______________________

____

Description	Quantity	Price
Leadership Lessons		**$16.95 each**
Shipping - $3.50 per order	TOTAL	
20% discount for orders of 10 or more books	Shipping	
	CA Sales tax (7.5%)	
	GRAND TOTAL	

Payment Method

☐ Check ☐ Money Order ☐ VISA ☐ MasterCard ☐ American Express

Expiration: ☐☐/☐☐

Card No: ☐☐☐☐ ☐☐☐☐ ☐☐☐☐ ☐☐☐☐

Name on Card: ______________________

Signature: ______________________

TO ORDER COPIES OF THIS BOOK, CALL OUR TOLL FREE NUMBER:
1-800-544-0414
OR COMPLETE THIS FORM AND FAX IT TO:
858-486-8595
OR EMAIL US AT: TOM@TOMHINTON.COM